May God bless your journey!

Love,

Bucky Morphew

INSPIRATIONAL MESSAGES ON

LIFE'S JOURNEY

BECKY MORPHEW

WESTBOW
PRESS®
A DIVISION OF THOMAS NELSON
& ZONDERVAN

WestBow Press books may be ordered through booksellers or by contacting:

WestBow Press
A Division of Thomas Nelson & Zondervan
1663 Liberty Drive
Bloomington, IN 47403
www.westbowpress.com
1 (866) 928-1240

ISBN: 978-1-5127-4334-0 (sc)
ISBN: 978-1-5127-4336-4 (hc)
ISBN: 978-1-5127-4335-7 (e)

Library of Congress Control Number: 2016908206

Print information available on the last page.

WestBow Press rev. date: 5/18/2016

I would like to dedicate this book first and foremost to my God who has always guided me and gave me the inspiration to minister the Word of God. To my wonderful husband, Tom, who always pushed me to accomplish all that God has for us. To our loving daughters, Lindsey and Jenna, who have always inspired me by their life's ambitions and their zeal for life. To our five grandchildren—Parker, Pax, Jadyn, Jake, and our little angel in heaven, Porter—who have each taught me how to appreciate the goodness of God and all of His blessings. To each of my family who have stood beside me with prayer and humor to continually motivate me to always do my very best. To all the people God has used in my life's journey to make me the person that I am today.

CONTENTS

CHAPTER 1

MESSAGES FROM GOD

This first chapter has messages that I believe came directly from God. I believe God gave each message, and He continues to speak today. We always need to hear what the Spirit is saying. My deep desire is for you to see how each of these messages can guide you on your life's journey.

The first message was about praise and entering into His holy presence. Entering into His presence requires us to first arise. Give God your praise and thanks. Focus your eyes and spirit on Him. Remove the blinders from your eyes. Stop stumbling around in the darkness. Walk into the courtyard, and fall at His feet. Sing and dance unto Him.

The blinders must come off! Your eyes will see His glory. The eyes of your soul look unto Him, but your physical eyes look unto the world. The world cannot provide for you. The world will keep you down in the pits. Remove the blindfolds from your spiritual eyes and arise. Come into His inner court.

Arise, children. Now is the time, and this is the season to rejoice. Now is the time and the season to remove all the cords that bind you and keep you from seeing the fullness of God. Come into His presence. See His glory! Arise, His children. Walk into His inner court, and fall at His feet. There is a time and a season for God's children to enter the throne room. It is the time to prepare you for what lies ahead. Place on your breastplates and your helmets, gird your loins, place the sword of God's Word between your lips, and prepare yourselves. Arise, God's children! Enter your appointed time. Prepare your minds, your hearts, and your souls for this time and this season. Arise. Seek God in all His glory. Let Him remove the blindfolds of darkness. Let Him open your eyes of enlightenment so that you may see the hope of His calling. Arise, and stand before God. He is the Alpha and the Omega.

Life's Journey Application

How can you use this message from God to change your life's journey? Are you standing in His presence or stumbling in the darkness?

. . . .

For God so loved the world that He gave His only begotten Son that whosoever believes in Him shall not perish but have everlasting life. (John 3:16 NKJV)

This message from God centers on each of us coming to Him and accepting His Son, Jesus, as our Lord and Savior.

The time is coming when God's children will follow Him with a greater compassion for others and for Him. They will have a greater love for God and a deeper thirst for His living waters. Watch for the signs. They surround you each day. Start expecting God's miracles and God's healings to surround your lives.

He is the true Vine, the great I Am. God will show each of His children that He is the only One who can bring true peace, joy, and comfort. His children must turn to Him like they never have before. Let Him enter your hearts. Let Him in. Do not delay.

Reach out for God is here. See Him for who He is. He will show you love that is greater than you have ever experienced before. God sent His only Son to earth to die for you. He saw you on the day that He hung on the cross. You were on His mind. You were and are the reason that God's Son died. Come with Him. He will show you what love is all about. Hear His words. Hear His voice. Walk with Him. Give Him praise and glory!

Life's Journey Application

Have you given your heart to Jesus? If you have never accepted Him into your heart and life, I pray that this is the day for your salvation.

. . . .

Have you ever been just minding your own business and all of a sudden, out of the clear blue sky, you hear a quiet voice that has such a magnitude that it becomes a deep, driving desire to fulfill His words? Well, it happened to me.

This is what I heard deep down within my spirit: *I can do the impossible, and the possible will happen.* My immediate response was "What?" However, as I sought God for the meaning, it started to become clearer that whatever the impossibilities are that are hindering our miracles, blessings, healings, and prayers, we must take a huge step in faith to receive our "possibles."

All our impossibilities can be turned around by faith, prayer, and total trust in God. Matthew 19:26 (NKJV) says, "With men this is impossible, but with God all things are possible."

The woman with the issue of blood for twelve years took an impossible step. She had strong faith and a total trust when she reached out in the crowd to touch the hem of Jesus's robe. She did the impossible—she touched Jesus's robe—and the possible happened to her. She received her healing!

What seems impossible in your life? Seek God, and He will show you how to turn the impossible into the possible. All of God's miracles begin with an impossible situation. The storms and setbacks of life are opportunities for us to trust God. God rewards those who diligently seek Him. We cannot attempt the impossible under our own strength. However, when we seek God in the midst of our impossible circumstances, He reveals His power and presence by accomplishing the impossible through us.

Life's Journey Application

I challenge each of you to attempt the impossible in your life, and God will make the possible happen.

Step 1: Do the impossible, and the possible will happen.

. . . .

Expect the Unexpected Favor of God

Now to Him who is able to do exceeding abundantly above all that we ask or think according to the power that works in us. (Ephesians 3:20 NKJV)

One of my favorite sayings is "Expect the unexpected favor of God!" My first thought each morning as I rise out of bed is *I can't wait to see what God is going to do in my life and the lives of others around me this day.* There have been some awesome prayers answered and unexpected favor on certain situations since I began expecting His favor. I expect His favor every moment of every day now! I give Him all the praise and glory.

Now my questions to each of you are these: What do you expect each day? Are you expecting God to do wonderful things, or are you living beneath a cloud of doubt, fear, and apprehension? We should always expect God to do the unexpected. We can expect, quite easily, for discouragements in our lives. We can easily believe that bad things will happen. There are some people reading this right now who have even thought about how bad the situation is in their lives. We tend to say, "What can happen next?" We believe that we live in a cause-and-effect world. We believe that if we continue to plan A, eventually it will result in plan B. But life doesn't always work that way. It is when we feel fear and apprehension that we need to expect God to do the unexpected.

We have nothing to lose by expecting God to do the unexpected in our lives. We may even discover that the unexpected exceeds our very own expectations. Remember, our expectations will determine our results. Expect the unexpected favor of God.

Life's Journey Application

Start this day believing God will do the unexpected in your life. Change your way of thinking and praying. Step back and see what the unexpected favor of God brings your way.

****

Life in the Word

Several years ago, I had a nightmare, the kind that wakes you up, sweating, your heart pounding, and you're scared. A dream that stays etched in your mind forever. Well, in this dream, I was with a group of Christians having a prayer service in a cold, dimly lit basement. The basement had about four long, rectangular windows with crisscrossed mesh wiring covering each window. As I led prayers, I heard the sound of marching soldiers coming down the sidewalk, just outside the basement's windows. I immediately told everyone to be very quiet and not utter a word. As we stood in complete silence, we saw soldiers' boots marching outside the basement windows. They were in search of Christians! They had been given the authority to kill anyone who had a Bible or was teaching others about the Bible.

As I awoke from this nightmare, I realized what an honor and privilege it is to live in a country where I can openly read and study my Bible and have the freedom to worship God.

During a weeklong power outage that we experienced with the ice storm of 2010, I was once again reminded of that nightmare. I was held hostage in my own bedroom by the grips of no electricity. As I lay there on the fifth day of the outage, my mind went back to that long-ago nightmare. I couldn't read my Bible. I couldn't write in my prayer and praise journal. I felt as if I were back in that dimly lit basement.

I thought, *I may not be able to read my Bible, but I know the Word.* So I began to recall as many Scriptures and Bible stories that I could remember. All of a sudden, the Word that I had placed in my heart from reading and studying my Bible came flooding back to me! Just when I thought I couldn't take this any longer, there was the Word of God to comfort me and to sustain me in literally the darkest nights I had ever experienced.

We must have the power of the Word to overcome the evilness and darkness of this world.

Life's Journey Application

Do you have enough Word in you to sustain you during your dark moments of life? Can you recall the Scriptures when you need them? If you answered no, I pray that you dust off your Bible and begin to earnestly read and study the words written just for you. Place the Word of God within your hearts. It will sustain you in your darkest moments.

. . . .

Encounter with God

Several weeks ago, I was awakened around 3 a.m. by my cell phone signaling a text message. Now no one likes to have their phones go off during the middle of the night, but this message was different. The text was from a friend (better be a friend at three in the morning). He had to share the revelation that God had just given him. Yes, God will talk to you at three in the morning. As I lay there after returning a text, I began praying for him and his situation.

Now, what happened next … I am not sure if I was in slight dream mode or if I was awake, but I felt the very presence of God Almighty enter our bedroom. The presence was so overwhelming! I can remember trying to shrink back from it. I wasn't afraid of it, but I felt that I was not worthy enough to be in the presence of Him. I felt dirty and tried to shield my face. My heart was beating so fast, but there was an overpowering feeling of peace.

The experience lasted only a short while, but I know I received a visitation from God that morning. Needless to say, I didn't get much sleep for the remainder of the night. Since the divine presence entered our room that morning, my life has changed so much. I know that God is preparing me to go out and preach and to use all that He has given me to fulfill my spiritual journey here on earth.

Life's Journey Application

Have you had an encounter with God? Draw closer to Him, and He will draw closer to you. Seek His face, and He will come.

. . . .

God Will Provide

I had a dream back in February 2013. Sometimes in my life, God gives me a dream that either foretells events or provides the solution to a certain problem. I believe that this dream had both of these elements within it. I pray that it will minister to you like it did for me.

In this dream, I was standing, looking out over the beautiful clear water of a peaceful sea. The sea was a long way down, so I was looking out over huge rocks and a very steep cliff. This is how we view life sometimes. Sometimes life is calm and beautiful, and other times it has huge rocks and tall, steep cliffs that are trying to block our sight. As I stood there looking out over the beautiful scene, I wanted to go for a swim in that gorgeous water; I always want to stay in the presence of God. However, to get to the water, I had to walk over an old rickety pier and climb down an old wooden ladder to get to the gorgeous water. The pier had many old boards that were sticking up that I had to dodge. The pier represents my life's journey on this earth. There were holes in some of the boards, representing heartaches that left huge holes in my heart. Some of the boards were swayed. I've had situations and crises in my life that may have swayed me and may have bent me, but through the love and grace of God, I still stood. Some of the boards were smooth but still rough and worn from age. Some were arched up and some were arched downward. Life's journey will sometimes be rough, with ups and downs, but through it all, God sustained me.

I made my way very carefully down the old pier and finally arrived at the wooden ladder. I had to climb very carefully to avoid the rusty nails that were protruding; sometimes we just have to dodge the Enemy's attacks against us. Finally, I reached the beautiful water and jumped in. It was so refreshing and calming. Whenever you enter the presence of God, there is nothing but peace and a refreshing restoration. God has taken me into His living waters many, many times and will continue to wash me with His living water.

I swam in the beautiful water for a long time. I did not want to leave, but I had to start making my way back to the ladder. As I swam toward the old ladder, it crumpled into the water with a loud crash. You can't go back to live in the past anymore; it's time to move forward and not turn back. So many of us live on the anointing and presence of God that happened to us yesterday, last month, or even last year. We need His anointing and presence every moment of our lives. No more living in your yesterdays. Move forward to your future.

In the dream, I was paddling to keep my head above the water when I realized that my only way out of the water was now gone. I panicked. What was I to do now? When life throws you into a panic, you will find yourself treading water to keep your head above the water. You will find yourself not knowing what to do or where to go. But if you'll be still and look around, God will provide a way. As I finally looked around in the water, I spotted a brand-new ladder that led up the high rocky cliff; God will always provide a way for you. As I made my way to the ladder, I remember praising God! I climbed the steep ladder all the way to the top. What a relief to know that God has all my steps covered and numbered.

As I took the final step off the ladder, I emerged on unfamiliar ground. I looked around, trying to see the exact point where I had entered the water on the long pier, but I couldn't locate it. God said, "You cannot go back. You cannot live in the past. You must move forward on new territory. I will guide you and prepare the way."

Life's Journey Application

Do you see yourself in this dream? Are you living in the past? Just remember that God has a plan for each of us, and He will guide our steps, whether we are walking on an old rickety pier, swimming in His holy presence, fearful of life's situations, or beginning to walk on our life's journey of new territory. God will provide.

****

Ringing of His Sweetness

As I was trimming trees on the back side of our land, I could hear our wind chimes blowing in the Oklahoma wind. When I stopped to take in the beautiful sound, I heard this beautiful, still, small voice whisper into me the following poem.

Hear the ringing of the bells.

Hear the beautiful chimes.

You, who have ears, hear.

Sound of My sweet melody,

Echoing through the land.

Do you hear His sweet call?

He is beckoning you in.

You, who have ears, hear.

A day soon the bells will stop,

The chimes of His sweetness

Will no longer be heard

Echoing through the land.

Hear—listen—now.

Before the ringing stops,

Make this sweetness

Known as Jesus your Savior today!

Life's Journey Application

If you do not know Jesus as your personal Lord and Savior, stop what you are doing right now and accept Him into your heart. Stop your delay; the day is coming when His sweet sound will no longer be heard ringing across this land.

****

God's Face Book

I awoke one morning with this swirling in my spirit: "to only have seen their faces." These are the faces—only some of them because there are so many—that belongs on God's face book.

Face = Features All Christ Encounters

I would have loved to see the faces of

> Moses when he came down from the mountain. Jesus's mother when He was born.

> The lady with the issue of blood when she was healed.

> Peter walking on the water.

> Noah when he looked up and saw all the animals coming onto the ark.

Mary when the angel told her she was going to have a Son.

Lazarus when he walked out of the tomb.

The little boy that gave his lunch to feed the five thousand.

Abraham when Sarah gave birth to Isaac.

Jacob when he saw his long lost son Joseph.

Adam and Eve when they walked and talked with God.

Joseph's brothers when they finally knew who Joseph was.

Blind Bartimeus when he could see.

The 120 people in the upper room when the Holy Ghost fell.

David's brothers when he killed Goliath.

The centurion when his daughter lived.

John the Baptist when he baptized Jesus.

Jesus when He died on the cross for my sins.

Jesus when He arose from the dead.

The disciplines when they realized that Jesus was really Jesus.

Oh, to see your faces when you are healed.

To see your faces when your marriages are restored.

To see your faces when your families are living for Jesus.

I will one day see the face of Jesus, and oh, I pray that He has a huge smile and speaks these precious Words, "Well done, My good and faithful servant."

Life's Journey Application

Which face do you want to see? Are you seeking the face of God, or are you just seeking what He can do for you? There is a difference. Start seeking His face, and you'll see a change in your walk with Him.

****

Chains Falling

Chains falling off! There is nothing like the feeling of being set free from the chains that have been holding us down.

I believe this day, God's daughters, He hears your weeping. He sees your tears. Today, you are standing on the very threshold of your miracle. Dry those tear-stained eyes and hearts, and listen to what the Spirit is saying. Know that this day you are standing on the verge of your miracle and deliverance. Your prayers are being heard and answered.

God has been speaking into my spirit for the last month about chains falling off. I can hear the sounds of chains falling to the floor and a newness falling upon you. I actually went to my husband's shop and found a chain in the cabinet. I picked it up and then I dropped it to the floor. It hit the floor with a clanging sound, the same sound that has been echoing in my ears. Chains are falling off the children of God! We are being set free from all that binds us.

I can hear some of you right now asking, "When? When will my chains fall? When will I be healed? When will my family be saved? When, when, when will all this happen?"

I know time seems to stand still when we are waiting on God for our miracles, our deliverances, and our prayers to be answered. It's all in His timing, not ours. God tells us to wait on Him. Waiting is something that we do not do well, but God says, "Wait."

Look at these examples from the Bible of how God's children had to wait. Their waiting turned into victories.

- The walls of Jericho took thirteen days before they fell. I'm telling you there is victory ahead.

- It took forty years before Joshua set foot on the land of milk and honey. Just remember that a long battle equals sweet blessings.

- Nahaum had to dip in the Jordan River seven times before he was healed. Obedience will equal answered prayers.

- Lazarus was dead for four days before Jesus called him back to life. We serve a living and all-powerful God. He is God of the impossible!

Life's Journey Application

What have you been praying for? Are you still waiting for your healing, your deliverance, your family's salvations, your miracle, or even your prayers to be answered? I tell you to wait on the Lord, trust, and have faith that the chains are falling away.

****

Be Prepared

This message I wrote in my quiet prayer time on the balcony, overlooking the beautiful ocean at Pensacola Beach, Florida.

As I was praying, deep within me I heard these words. Look at all of God's beauty! His people need to surround themselves in His creation and in His presence. For He has created all things, both small and great. Look to His beauty; come and enjoy the fullness of Him.

God knows each sand pebble that blankets this shore. He knows each drop of salty water that washes ashore. He knows the weight and strength of each pounding wave. He knows the timing of each wave that ripples across the vastness of the ocean. He knows every fish and every creature that swims below the deep blue waters. If He knows and has created all of this, how come you don't know that God can do all things and that he is all things?

It's time to throw off the heaviness that clings to us like pebbles of white sand. He gives the spirit of gladness and happiness. Come to Him all of you who are heavy laden. Dry off the leftover water from your body because God is cleansing you with brand-new water—His water—the living water. Once you have tasted His water, you'll never be thirsty again.

We must wait for His perfect timing. Just like the waves, all things work together for good, and His timing is perfect! Seek Him first, and He will show you where and what you are to do. Don't get ahead of Him or fall behind Him.

The force of the waves will knock you down if you're not prepared for them. Be prepared at all times for the Enemy to try to catch you off guard. The Enemy will hit with violent force and send you tumbling down, but God will help you back up. Stand strong, and be on guard about your surroundings. Stay prepared and watchful! Jesus is coming; Jesus is coming for those who are looking for Him. Be ready, be prepared, and be strong.

Life's Journey Application

On this day, take a look at your life, inside and out. See if there is anything that needs some extra attention. God can show you and take away each burden and spirit of heaviness. Wash this day in the water of God, and start experiencing all the fullness of God.

. . . .

Self-Evaluation on Life's Journey

One must continue to grow and learn each day. If you are not growing and learning, you are not moving forward on your journey. Take a few moments and answer the following self-evaluation questions to see what you have learned about yourself.

1. How have these inspirational messages from God motivated you to seek a change in your life?

2. If you have felt a need to change anything in your life, what is the one area that you need to pray and seek God's help in changing?

3. Has your life's journey changed in any way?

****

Notes from Chapter 1

****

CHAPTER 2

CRISIS IN THE JOURNEY

Living in Victory

> These things I have spoken to you, that in Me you may have
> peace. In the world you will have tribulation; but be of good
> cheer, I have overcome the world. (John 16:33 NKJV)

Have you ever felt like you were on top of the mountain one moment
and in the deep, dark despair of the valley the very next moment? This
is only a short form of victory. Yet, if we take Jesus at His every Word,
we should be victorious all the time.

Jesus gave us a very important insight into His message to His disciples
the night He spoke these words. We need to have an eternal outlook on
our lives and the things that are happening in our life's journey. We need
to persevere and have faith when we are facing trials and tribulations.
We need to be dedicated to our prayer life and boldly come before the
throne of God. Jesus told us that we could ask for anything in His name.
We need to be confident that Jesus is with us, learn to depend on Him,

and seek Him. We need to make Him our only example to follow. We need to be purified of our sins and live and abide within Him.

Today, don't just stand still and let the Enemy have what is rightfully yours. Don't be content with defeat or failure, but know that God wants you to have a permanent victory and the sweet peace that only He can give. Fill your mind with the Word of God and then put His Word into practice in your life. Speak His promises over your situations. The Word will never come back void. If the Bible says it, believe it! Trust Him with everything that you have, and He will reward you. Believe in Him because He'll never leave or forsake you. Depend on the guidance of the Holy Spirit in your life. Pray boldly and with authority. God has given you the authority over the Enemy and all his tactics. Persevere and have faith that you will overcome. Start believing for the victories in your life.

Life's Journey Application

Pray this prayer over yourself and your situation this day.

· ·

Lord, I will not accept defeat in my life starting this day. I will believe You for a permanent victory in my life. Lord, thank You for sending Your only Son to overcome this world. Thank You, Lord, for this victory. I may not see it with my physical eyes, but I am seeing it with my spiritual eyes. I declare complete victory in every area of my life. Thank You, Jesus.

· ·

When Your Back Is Against the Wall

Praise the Lord! "Let everything that has breath praise the Lord" (Psalm 150:6 NKJV).

Have you ever had just a small verse of a song go around and around in your head? For the last several months, I can hear these words echoing in my mind over and over: "When your back is against the wall, praise the Lord." I know from experience that this is the hardest time to praise the Lord. It will probably be one of the hardest things to do because praises are not exactly what is on your mind. However, this is the time we need to praise Him the most.

We have all been in circumstances that seem unbearable. We see no way out. We actually feel like our backs are against a hard, unmoving wall.

This is the moment our eyes and praises need to look up to our heavenly Father. He will bring us through the unbearable circumstance. In Daniel 3:19 (NKJV), the Word tells a remarkable story of three Hebrew boys, Shadrach, Meshach, and Abed-Nego, who were thrown into a fiery furnace. Their situation looked impossible. Their circumstance was unbearable. They definitely had their backs against a fiery wall. The Word says the boys fell down in the midst of the fiery furnace. Could they have been praising God? God immediately showed up and saved them from their unbearable circumstance. He did it for the three Hebrew boys, and He can and will do it for each of us.

Just remember when your back is against the wall, praise the Lord. He will walk you out of your fiery furnace. He promised to never leave or forsake us.

Life's Journey Application

What fiery furnace has you against the wall? Start this day praising God, and watch Him walk into your situation and change the temperature of the fire. I challenge you to put a song of praise upon your lips.

****

Crisis Comes to All of Us

All things are possible to those who believe in the Lord. We must look beyond where we are with the eyes of faith, believing God for even the impossible.

When tragedies fall upon your family, you feel so helpless. We had been going through a fire with an accident that happened to one of our family members. Our pastor said, "When someone else is going through the fire, it is a situation. But when you are going through the fire, it is a crisis. We have been operating in crisis mode. We know that God is still in full control at all times. We have felt His presence. We have seen His hands touch and heal. We have felt His presence when we were down. We serve a mighty God who can and will do all things for His children.

Our crisis started several weeks ago when my husband's brother had an accident that landed him in an ICU in Fort Worth, Texas. As we walked into his room, the feeling of hopelessness tried to overcome us, but we knew that we had to stand strong, not only for ourselves, but for the rest of the family.

We don't plan on life throwing us into desperate times and situations, but sometimes that is exactly what happens. Your entire life can change in a blink of an eye. That is why we need to make sure that we are prepared at all times to face these crises. The only way we got through his stay in the hospital was to lean upon God, and trust and believe that all would fine.

When life throws you into a medical crisis and life-and-death situation, seek the Lord for His strength and healing powers.

Life's Journey Application

This was my prayer during that time. "Lord, help me as I go through this medical tragedy. Help me, Lord, to stand strong in You. Guide me, Lord, in every decision that I will be required to make. Give me Your strength to endure endless nights at the hospital. Lord, send Your healing touch upon my loved one that so desperately needs a healing miracle. Lord, I thank You and praise You for carrying us at this time. Amen."

. . . .

Loss of a Loved One

> Do not let your heart be troubled; believe in God, believe also in Me. In My Father's house are many dwelling places, if it was not so, I would have told you, for I go to prepare a place for you. If I go and prepare a place for you, I will come again and receive you to Myself, that where I am, there you may be also. (John 14:1–3 NASB)

There comes a time in everyone's life when Jesus says that it is time to come home to be with Him in heaven. Last week, our family once again experienced the loss of one of our dear family members. My husband's brother entered heaven's gates! Death is always so hard and appears to be so final, but we as Christians know that life here on earth is like a blink of the eye compared to an eternal life in heaven. We can have peace and hope in knowing that our loved ones stepped over to be with Jesus forever and forever. We can know beyond a shadow of a doubt that they now are completely healed with no pain or sorrow.

How do we know this? Many people question why we should think about heaven at all. But Jesus answered that question in His teaching the night He was betrayed. He knew that we would have problems and pains in this life, but He said we must not let our hearts be troubled. Instead, we should believe in Him, have faith in His Word, and trust Him to provide peace and strength during our times of grief.

As our thoughts focus on heaven, we realize that He hasn't forgotten us. Rather, he has prepared a glorious place for us. We should think about heaven as our Father's house filled with many dwelling places. Dwelling places where we and our loved ones will live forever. And Jesus has promised to come for us, so we can be with Him forever.

Now, you and I may be prepared to meet Jesus, but how about our friends, loved ones, coworkers, and the person who sits beside you at church. Yes, I said church. You can go to church on a regular basis and still not be saved. Ask yourself these questions. Do they know how to get to heaven? Do they know Jesus as their personal Lord and Savior? We as Christians have a calling to put Matthew 28:19 into practice with those around us: "Go therefore and make disciples of all the nations, baptizing them in the Name of the Father, Son and of the Holy Spirit." We have been commissioned to spread the gospel to the entire world.

What are you waiting for?

Life's Journey Application

Have you ever experienced the loss of a loved one? If you have, you know how hard this time of grief and sorrow can be. But take note that Jesus can give you His peace that passes all understanding. You will see them again, so hold on and be strong. Just be patient; each of us grieves in different ways.

. . . .

Jesus, What's in a Name

This article was written by my husband, Tom, when I was diagnosed with breast cancer. I had just started chemo treatments and was facing many rounds of chemo and thirty-three rounds of radiation treatments.

In the last several weeks, Becky and I have been traveling back and forth to see her cancer doctor. As each of you know, every doctor's office has a waiting room. While we waited and waited for our turn to see the doctor, we read magazines, watched TV, and looked at every picture and plaque on the wall. One particular plaque kept drawing my eyes toward it. I kept studying the small wooden plaque, but I couldn't figure out what it was about. It was a wooden plaque with smaller pieces of wood stacked in different directions. As I kept studying the plaque, all of a sudden, it became as plain as day. It was right there in front of me. I didn't tell Becky about the plaque that day. I didn't tell her how the boldness of the message jumped out at me. However, the following week, I noticed Becky looking at the plaque. She finally asked me, "What does that plaque say?"

I told her, "Can't you see, Jesus?" The name of Jesus was right there as plain as day. Then she saw the bold name of Jesus standing out on the wooden plaque. Jesus is always there right in front of us. Sometimes we can't see Him for all the things that are going on around us. But He is always there; we just have to keep looking forward and keep our focus on Him. He will guide us through life's detours and bumps. I know that everything is going to be all right because Jesus is there for both of us. Just trust and lean upon Him.

Life's Journey Application

If you are going through cancer or any type of sickness, know that you can put your trust in God. He will hold your hand and still your fears. I know because this is what He did for me. I pray for you right now that whatever illness you are going through, that by the stripes of Jesus, you are healed. I may have had to go through the cancer treatments, but I am now eight years cancer-free. Just because you have to go through the medical test and treatments doesn't mean that God is not working.

. . . .

Faith will see you through the storms of life!

Our God calls us sometimes to do impossible things by our faith so He can receive glory. We should always keep our eyes on Jesus in every part of our lives. Our eyes must stay focused on Him even when the storms of life are battering you against the wall. Please take the time to read Matthew 14:22–33 (NKJV). This point is completely illustrated in these verses. The verses tell us that the disciples had a long, tiring day, and Jesus sent them out in the boat to go to another town. When we get physically, mentally, and spiritually tired, our faith seems to weaken, and we are not prepared to face the storms of life as we should. We must keep ourselves full of the Word, stay in constant prayer, and get physical rest.

Now the story continues with the disciplines out in a boat on a dark, stormy night. The wind was tossing the waves around, and the disciples were being thrown all over the ship. In the middle of the night, they thought they were seeing a ghost when Jesus came to them, walking on the sea! When we are in darkness or a storm of life, things may appear to be distorted or not what they really are. However, Jesus saw they were scared and told them not to be afraid. When they were the most afraid, He told them to cheer up; He was with them. He will never leave you or forsake you. God has to take the storms out of us before He can take us out of the storms of life.

Peter must have wondered if it was really Jesus or just his imagination. He asked Jesus to tell him to come out on the water with Him. Jesus didn't say, "I'm sorry. Peter, but water-walking is for Messiahs only." Instead, He said one simple word: "Come." God calls us to do impossible things by faith. It must have taken a lot of faith for Peter to take that first step out of the boat in the middle of the wind, waves, and the storm. When he did, Peter walked on water! The Bible says in Matthew 14:29 (NKJV), "And when Peter had come down out of the ship, he walked on the water, to go to Jesus. But when he saw the wind boisterous, he was afraid; and began to sink, he cried, saying 'Lord, save me.'" Peter was doing fine until he took his eyes off Jesus. As long as he had faith, he did the impossible with God's help. He kept his eyes on Jesus and walked on water. When he looked around at the world, he started believing that the storms were going to defeat him. He lost faith. He took his eyes off Jesus and began to sink. If we forget that Jesus is right there to help us, we can let the storms of life cause us to sink. If we keep our eyes on Jesus, we can do mighty things by our faith.

Then Peter uttered what is probably the shortest prayer in the Bible: "Lord, save me." Everyone needs to say that prayer. We all need Jesus to save us. He is our only hope. Jesus told Peter he should not have doubted.

When they got back on the boat, everyone came and worshipped Jesus, saying, "Truly You are the Son of God." We must always remember to give God the praise and glory for each storm that He has taken us through.

Life's Journey Application

Lord, my prayer this day is for You to help me keep my eyes focused upon You. Help me, Lord, to always remember to give You praise and glory for each storm that You have brought me through. Lord, when I get afraid and feel like I am sinking, pull me up, and hold me until I can refocus on You.

****

Life's Challenging Situations

> If you would earnestly seek God and make your supplication to the Almighty, If you were pure and upright, surely now He would awake for you and prosper your rightful dwelling place. (Job 8:5–6 NKJV)

Life has a unique way of bringing challenging situations into our lives. Sometimes we allow them to overcome us and penetrate every part of our lives. Sometimes during these challenging situations we even allow the spirit of depression to overtake us and affect our happiness and joy.

Such was the case of Elijah in 1 Kings 19 (NKJV). Elijah was facing a very difficult challenge in his life. He had allowed this difficult situation to turn his life into one of fear, anxiety, and depression. The fear and depression consumed every part of Elijah's life.

Are you facing a very difficult challenge in your life? Have you allowed the spirit of depression to overcome you during this challenge?

In the beginning of chapter 19, we find a very depressed and defeated Elijah, sitting under a broom tree, all alone in his fear and depression. I can just hear Elijah asking God these two questions: "How did I get here?" and "How did I get to where I am?" Maybe you have been going through a situation and have asked these same questions.

Just remember there are three kinds of people in this world: those who are in the middle of the wilderness (going through a challenging situation), those who just came out of the wilderness (the challenging situation is finally over), and those who are headed into the wilderness (a challenging situation is ahead of them.) Everyone is going through something.

In the mist of Elijah's wilderness experience, God sent His angel to feed Elijah. God will give you strength during your times of weakness. In 1 Kings 19:7 (NKJV), God told him, "Arise and eat because the journey is too great for you." Elijah responded, "What journey? I'm through." God spoke to Elijah, telling him that he was not through. God was going to send him from where he was to where God wanted him to be. God was going to send Elijah from the wilderness to the mountain. God can take you from the wilderness to the mountaintop in your challenging situations. Just hold on and trust Him.

Life's Journey Application

In the wilderness there is weakness, but on the mountain is strength. In the wilderness there is despair, but on the mountain there is hope!

God can and will help in each challenging situation in your life. God can take away that spirit of depression and set you on a fresh start in life. Just turn it over to Him.

. . . .

Now faith is the substance of things hoped for, the evidence of things not seen. (Hebrews 11:1 NKJV)

"Wow" and "double wow" are words that could be used to describe our life a few years back. Have you ever experienced that? Tom and I have two brand-new grandsons. What a blessing! One of our grandsons was born with a heart defect (heterodoxy syndrome), which means in very simple terms that some of his heart plumbing is defected. The doctors are amazed that he is still with us. We all know he is because we serve a mighty God and the great healer!

I want to tell you a story about our daughter, Jenna, and her three-year-old son about his little brother's heart problem. She was telling him that Porter's heart was broken and needed to be fixed. To which he replied, "Doesn't he have Jesus in his heart?" Oh, childlike faith. You see, Parker already knew that Jesus can do all things if we just have faith and believe that with Jesus in our hearts, all things are possible.

Ephesians 3:20 (NKJV) reads, "Now to Him who is able to do exceeding abundantly above all that we ask or think according to the power that works in us." We must have faith and believe that with God all things are possible. But we must do our part and ask and think with the power that works in us. Our faith and high expectations will take us forward into the presence of the living God we serve. We must believe for the very best that God will and can do. He will give His very best, but we have to be expecting it

Life's Journey Application

No matter what roller-coaster ride your life seems to be on right now, allow the power of the almighty God to see you through. Believe with childlike faith that God will take care of all things. Look beyond where you are, and see with the eyes of faith, believing God for even the impossible. Impossibles are completely dissolved when we look with our faith eyes and know that our Redeemer lives.

. . . .

I Still Believe

Have you ever been deep down in the valley? Have you ever received news that was so devastating that it immediately consumed every fiber of your being? Have you ever been to the point in your life where fears try to overtake you?

I know that several of you reading this are nodding your heads right now. You've been down in the valley. You've received devastating news. You've been to the point where fear consumed and overtook you.

We all go through these dark valleys at certain points in our earthly journeys. We may not fully understand them or the plan or purpose for them, but we still must walk through them. There is no going around them; we must go through them.

We received devastating news concerning our grandson, Porter. The heart doctors had told us that there was nothing more than they could do to save our precious little grandson. It was not what we had prayed and believed for. As I sought God that night, He wrapped me in His arms and reminded me of this Scripture in Hebrews 13:5 (NKJV): "I will never leave you or forsake you." I believe that I cried a river that night, curled up in my heavenly Father's arms. I took strength in Him.

Now I did ask myself (yes, I talk to myself, and I even answer myself sometimes), "Do I just quit believing God? Quit believing in His Word? Quit believing what I teach and preach?" And the answer was no!

With God's grace and mercy, we will go through the valley. God is still on the throne. God is still the great I Am!

I will continue to believe, expect, and praise God. I will continue to believe and expect God's mighty hand to use this valley for His glory.

Life's Journey Application

What have you done when you're faced with devastating news? Have you stepped back to examine it closer to see God's plan and purpose for it? I pray that whenever these moments come in your life's journey, God gives you His peace and strength to go through the valley and emerge on the next mountain.

Sorrows … God Will Heal

Things happen in this world that we do not understand. We ask why, but we receive no answers. We know that all things happen for a reason and a purpose, but it doesn't make it any easier to go through them.

I say this with tears streaming down my face because our little grandson, Porter, is now in the arms of Jesus. He was a miracle that God loaned us for a short time. We will miss him so much, but the great thing is that we will see him again.

We sometimes feel like we are surrounded by a huge wall of questions that are left unanswered. We seek guidance and direction in the wee hours of the night. We seek for the answers in our hearts. We search for a reason. We find moments of strength and peace in God. Moments that will continue to grow longer second by second, minute by minute, hour by hour, day by day, month by month, and year by year. Those moments sent directly from heaven are our lifelines from God to help us in our times of unanswered questions and hearts that are saddened.

We know that the Word says in Psalm 34:18 (NIV), "The Lord is close to the brokenhearted and saves those who are crushed in spirits." These words are a lifeline thrown to us to help scale the walls of unanswered questions and sadness. As we suffer, we must remember these truths.

1. God does not abandon us when we suffer, although it often feels as if He does. No, He has been with us, will be with us, and is always with us.

2. The presence of hardship does not mark the absence of God. A broken heart is irresistible to Him. God comes to the brokenhearted.

3. God does not promise to protect us from all problems, but He does promise to be with us through our problems.

4. Adversity will either come between you and God, or it will push you closer to God. In times of intense sadness, we must turn to Him, and we must encourage our friends and family members to do likewise. When we do so, our Father comforts us, and in time, He heals us.

Life's Journey Application

So, while we wait on the Lord to heal our broken hearts, we will continue to praise His mighty name. We will continue to pray and believe in His Word. There will be a day when the unanswered questions that have been written on the huge walls of our lives will no longer need to be answered. The answers will no longer matter when we are standing with our precious loved ones in heaven, singing praises to our Father!

If you have lost a loved one and your questions are still unanswered, trust in God that you, just like us, will find peace. Our loved ones are waiting for us just beyond the pearly gates.

****

Holes in My Heart

As I was praying and preparing for this month's newsletter article, my thoughts continued to return to the sadness and grief that have left holes in so many of our hearts. We have felt and experienced the overwhelming moments of unbearable sorrow and grief in losing one of our precious loved ones. These holes in our hearts will have an effect on our lives and, in essence, change each of us forever. The loss of a family member not only affects you but affect each person in the family in totally different ways. I just wanted to let you know if there is a hole in your heart, it's all right to feel sadness. You may even feel and handle the process in totally different ways that the rest of your family, and that's all right. There is no set or right way to mourn; each person will handle each step of the grieving process in different ways. There are no time limitations on the grieving process. We need to know that although we live in a time world, the actual grieving process differs from person to person.

One thing that I do know about each of us during these times is we are each left with holes in our hearts. Some are huge, gaping holes, and some are small ones. I also know these holes left on our hearts will affect and change each of our lives forever.

As we are being affected and changed by these painful times, I have found from past holes in my heart that we must look to God for His peace and strength. He will guide you when you can't guide yourself. He will restore you with His peace. He will listen to your cries, hear your sorrow, and hold the holes in your heart in the palms of His almighty hands. Psalm 142:1–2, 5–6 (NIV), reads, "I cry aloud to the Lord; I lift up my voice to the Lord for mercy. I pour out my complaint before Him; before Him I tell my trouble … I cry to You, O Lord; I say You are my refuge, my portion in the land of the living. Listen to my cry, for I am in desperate need." We must look to God for our help. He will be your Rock during these times.

As time goes forward, the holes in our hearts may lessen, but they are still there. They are always a part of us, Touching and shaping us as we continue on life's journey.

I wrote this poem last March, when I was experiencing hurt, unbelievable sorrow, and uncontrollable grief over the huge hole that was left in my heart when our grandson, Porter, went home to see Jesus.

God looked at the day,

So calm and bright.

But down in my heart sadness grows.

It lingers hidden,

Hidden within my heart.

My heart has a huge hole

That seems like it will never close.

God, do You hear me?

Please touch my broken heart.

Mend it, hold it, and piece it.

Piece it one piece at a time.

Oh, God, where is my joy?

Hidden under all this sorrow,

It's fighting to emerge,

Struggling to return.

Oh, God, at last I seem to feel

Your holy, peaceable presence.

A strong presence and gentle touch

Amid my broken heart.

Slow, small trickles of Your healing power

That consume and restore

Piece by piece

My grieving heart!

Life's Journey Application

My prayer for each of you is that God continues to mend the holes in your hearts. May He give each of you His peace that surpasses all understanding. May He use these experiences in your life to touch, mold, and shape you to what He needs for your life's journey. May He pour out His healing powers upon your shattered hearts.

I also pray that each of you know Jesus as your Lord and Savior because there will be an awesome day when the holes in our hearts are completely mended. The very moment we step into the loving arms of Jesus, the holes will be gone forever. We will be at that precise moment without tears, pain, grief, or sorrow. We will once again see all our lost loved ones who have left these huge holes in our hearts. May God bless each of you, and may He hold you in the palms of His hands.

. . . .

"Arise Up Out of the Ashes"

You never know who you are in God until you have been through the fire of life. You will never know how much God has worked in your life until He raises you out of the ashes of that fiery situation.

Everyone has either stood in amid a raging fire or walked through the flames of an out of control fire on our life's journey. The facts is you are either getting ready to walk in a fire, standing in a fire, or coming out of a fire.

On July 6, my family was once again going through a mighty fire. This particular date and the importance of it was and still amazes me for how great our God is, was, and will be. You see, this was supposed to have been our precious grandson Porter's first birthday, but we didn't get to celebrate it with him. Instead, he had the honor of celebrating it with Jesus! I had full intentions of having a pity party all day, but God had other plans. He gave me the message of "Standing in the Fire" moments after I got up that morning. I minister that message to not only myself but to many others who had been standing in the fire.

The beginning of the message that He gave me over two years ago went like this. The fires that we walk through in our life's journey resemble the same characteristics of a real fire. They each will burn you. They will try to destroy you. They can and will consume you. They will not stop there; they will also consume all that is in their paths. Some of the fires are easy to put out, but some are huge, raging wildfires that seem to go on forever, consuming every part of you, physically, emotionally, and spiritually. The wildfires will consume you unless you keep your eyes focused on God. He will see you through the fires again and again.

Do you walk and stand by your faith when you are in the fire? Do you believe in God even in the midst of your pain and suffering? Do you believe in the promises of God even when everything looks impossible? Do you trust Him even when you do not understand His ways and His workings in your live? The depth of our faith in God is revealed when we are standing in the fires of trials and tribulations. First Peter 1:6–7 (NKJV) says, "In this you greatly rejoice, though now for a little while, if need be, you have been grieved by various trials, that the genuineness of your faith, being much more precious than gold that perishes, though it is tested by fire, may be found to praise, honor, and glory at the revelation of Jesus Christ."

The next July 6, God gave me a new message: "Arise up out of the Ashes." How awesome that God spoke so directly with me on two different birthdays to help me, to show me, to direct me, and to renew my faith. You will never know who you are in Christ until you have been in the fire. You will never know how God has worked in your life until He raises you out of the ashes.

It's time to rise from the ashes of fire that have consumed your life. Ashes are the remains of a fire, the evidence of destruction, the substance remaining after something has been burned, the bleak darkness of your reality, your life, your journey. Are you sitting in the ashes? Have you been consumed by a recent fire and are still sitting in the ashes of your destruction? Time to arise out of the ashes!

When the landscape has been consumed by a raging fire, we look at it and see deadness, darkness, and destruction. The landscape will sit like that for a while in all of its deadness, but wait! Finally, something starts to happen. The physical rain begins to fall upon the barrenness of the leftover destruction, and suddenly, we start to notice a change. Arising out of the ashes is new life! The grass begins to grow greener than ever.

Fire, as ugly as it was, deposited necessary nutrients into the soil of the landscape, and what was darkness has changed because out of the ashes arise grass and thriving landscape. It is alive and bigger and better that before. Arise out of the ashes!

We can do the same. Arise to a new life out of the ashes. When we have been in the fires of this life's journey, God's nutrients are being deposited into our spirits to sustain us through the darkness, the destruction, and the bleakness. When the fires are gone, we are equipped by His mercy and grace to arise out of the ashes stronger and more alive than ever before. Isaiah 61:1–4 (NKJV) tells about beauty for ashes. There are several keys words in Isaiah 61 that describes the very process of rising from the ashes, to heal, to proclaim, opening prison doors, to comfort, to console, to give them beauty for ashes, oil of joy, garment of praise, the planting of the Lord, rebuild, raise, and repair are for us now. This day I believe and expect a spiritual renewing arising out of the ashes for you.

Life's Journey Application

How long have you been sitting in the aftermath of a wildfire? Read Isaiah 61:1–4 (NKJV) over and over until you get the meaning deep within your spirit. God's Word will guide you through the process of going from standing in the fire to arising out of the ashes. Make sure you receive beauty for your ashes.

. . . .

All Is Well

All is well! All is well! We must live by these three little words: All is well! These words came into my spirit when I needed to hear them. I've never forgotten them and the important lesson that I learned through the entire experience. *All is well,* was spoken into my spirit about five and a half years ago. The season in my life was scary, dark, and crazy. I had just discovered a lump in my breast and was preparing for a biopsy to determine if the lump was cancer. God in all His wisdom dropped the story of Elisha and the Shummite woman into my spirit. The three amazing words all is well were amplified as I read the story. The very same day God sent even more confirmation by one of His servants. The e-mail stated, "When I was praying for you, all that I can hear God say is, all is well."

The words of God carried me through the biopsy and through the dreaded word "cancer," chemo, and thirty-three radiation treatments. All was well in my spirit even when my physical eyes saw differently. My faith eyes saw me healed and over the journey of cancer. God has used this part of my journey to share with others that God is still alive and well, and His Word is truth.

God is so faithful to us! All is well. May each of you reading this retain in your heart these three words, and may they echo through your mind and settle into your hearts. May you have all is well in every situation in your life.

In 2 Kings 4:8–37 (NKJV) the Shummite woman used her eyes of faith. We must do the same; we must look beyond where we are and see with the eyes of faith, believing that all is well. All is well in the presence of God. He will never leave us or forsake us.

I have been asked many times, "Do you really believe those three little words, all is well?" Yes, I always answer with a simple smile. God is still on the throne, and I know that I know!

When you get this all is well deep into your spirit, you will experience a joy that surpasses all understanding. We must remember whenever we face any type of adversity in our lives not to lose our joy. Hold onto it. The joy of the Lord is my strength. Rejoice in the Lord always! Wait, how do we rejoice, have joy, even believe that all is well when we face trouble? Because we know that the trying of our faith works patience and brings us into God's perfect and entire plan for us. Paul stated, "I know whom I have believed." In the book of Job, around chapter 19 (NKJV), Job said, "My Redeemer lives." Job declared his faith amid adversity. We sometimes miss the joy part of our faith.

All is well; all is well. We need to sing praises to Him. We need to clap our hands. We need to dance like David in the holy presence of our God. Keep those praises on your lips all day long. Praise Him even when you do not feel like praising Him. I admit this is sometimes very hard to do, especially when life takes an unexpected turn. When fear floods over you, when hopelessness appears on the horizon, when our backs are against the wall, when doubt creeps in and settles over every inch of our bodies, when the Enemy corners us to attempt to kill, steal, and destroy us. Put your praise garments on! Believe God, hold fast to your faith, and feed upon His Word. He will strengthen us in every situation.

All is well; all is well!

Life's Journey Application

First Samuel chapter 30 (NKJV) tells of David strengthening himself in the Lord. Encourage yourself in the Lord. Keep His praises flowing from your mouth and your lips at all times. Ask Him for His guidance, His wisdom, and strength. Don't stay in the pit too long. Arise, and start walking with the One who will carry you if needed. Our life situations will begin changing in His presence and with our praises. Psalm 30 (NKJV) says, "Weeping may endure for a night, but joy comes in the morning!" God will take our mourning and turn it into joy.

****

Put Your Armor On!

Ephesians 6:10-18

As I was seeking God for an article, my spirit kept going back to the one I wrote for the October 2012 newsletter, which was titled "Put Your Armor On." I feel like this article needs to be reprinted. Why? Because we are living in the end times, and the Enemy is roaring against the saints from every direction. We need to be on guard and make sure that we are wearing our armor at all times. We cannot afford to take off our armor. We simply need to do some readjusting as necessary.

It is time for the Enemy to be crushed and stopped in every area of our lives, faith, families, finances, and futures. We must take a bold stance! Now is not the time to sit down, turn away, or give up. We must make a stand as children of the Most High God. Ephesians 6:10–18 (NKJV) tells each of us how to stand against the Enemy. God tells us in His Word exactly what we need to do to overcome the Enemy and keep him from every area of our lives. "Finally, my brethren, be strong in the Lord and in the power of His Might. We cannot do this ourselves. We must have Jesus and the power of the Holy Spirit. Put on the whole armor of God that you may be able to stand against the wiles of the devil." Satan's tricks and attempts to defeat us in our daily lives can be avoided when we wear the armor of God. "For we do not wrestle against flesh and blood, but against principalities, against powers, against the rulers of the darkness of this age, against spiritual hosts of wickedness in the heavenly places." The Enemy wants to kill, steal, and destroy us. He knows that his time is short-lived, so he is working overtime. "Therefore, take up the whole armor of God that you may be able to withstand in the evil day, and having done all to stand." The evil days are upon us! The closer that it gets to Jesus coming back, the harder the battle against us. "Stand, therefore, having girded your waist with truth."

In John 17:17 (NKJV) we find, "Jesus spoke, sanctify them in Your truth. Your Word is truth." Truth means to have integrity, a life of practical truthfulness and honestly. "Having put on the breastplate of righteousness." The righteousness breastplate is the practical righteous character and deeds of the believers. "And having shod your feet with the preparation of the gospel of peace." This verse can mean two things. the gospel is the firm foundation on which Christians are to stand and live our lives. We must stand on the Word of God. The second meaning means we as Christians should be ready to go out to defend and spread the gospel. "Above all, taking the shield of faith with which you will be able to quench all the fiery darts of the wicked one." The shield is to be used to cover all areas of your life. Our shield offers protection against the constant attacks from the Enemy. "And take the helmet of salvation." We must have our helmets on to protect our heads and our minds against the Enemy's attacks. "And the sword of the spirit which is the Word of God." The sword is the only offensive weapon in the whole armor. This weapon is not necessarily the whole Bible but the specific Word or Scriptures that need to be spoken in a specific situation. To have the precise Word ready, a person must know the Bible intimately. "Praying always with prayer and supplication in the Spirit." We must pray and pray without ceasing! "Being watchful to this end with all perseverance and supplication for all the saints."

I have been praying the following prayer daily for three years over readjusting my armor. I pray that you will also start praying this prayer for your own armor.

> Heavenly Father, I praise and worship You because You are God. I am honored to be Your servant, and I take my stand today against the Devil and his schemes against me, my family, and my ministry. Father, as I readjust each piece of armor, please secure it in place on me.
>
> I take up the shield of faith and extend it over myself. It extinguishes all the fiery darts of the Evil One. I put on the helmet of salvation, which protects my mind from the Enemy's attack. I have the mind of Christ. I put on the breastplate of righteousness, which covers my body with the righteousness of God. In Christ, every foothold of evil has been washed away, and I am clothed in righteousness!
>
> I gird my loins with the belt of truth. Your Word, oh God, is truth! Father, sanctify me according to Your Word, and remind me through the Holy Spirit of the truth that destroys the schemes of the Enemy.
>
> I shod my feet with the preparation of the gospel of peace. I have peace with God and peace with humankind. I walk in my inheritance as an adopted child of the Most High God. I have authority over Evil in Jesus's name.
>
> I will use the sword of the Spirit by speaking the Word of God as it applies to whatever situation I may face today. Father, please remind me of Your Word through the Holy Spirit. I will continue to pray in the Spirit throughout the day and intercede

for all as the Holy Spirit prompts me. I believe that the Holy Spirit is interceding on my behalf according to my prayers.

Thank You, Father, for the whole armor of God. Please surround me with Your hedge of protection as I move forward on this spiritual battlefield. I praise and worship You now and forever. Amen.

Life's Journey Application

Start making your stand today against the Enemy and all his tricks and tactics. Get your armor on, just like you put your clothes on each morning. Make a spiritual effort to readjust your spiritual clothing. You will begin to notice a change in the atmosphere around you when you are armed with God's armor. Pray this prayer each morning over yourself and over your family and friends. It works!

****

Self-Evaluation on Life's Journey

1. How have these messages on Personal Crisis touched your life?

2. Which personal crisis can you identify with in your life? Has it influenced or motivated you to make a necessary change?

3. After reading and applying the messages to my life, what will I need to focus on. I will seek God's direction and guidance to become an overcomer!

****

Notes from Chapter 2

****

CHAPTER 3

NEW BEGINNINGS

Financial Freedom

Financial freedom can be found even in the worst economic mess. The world's principles of financial freedom are so different than God's principles of financial freedom. I discovered this godly principle in 2003. I discovered what the principle of sowing, watering, and harvesting into God's kingdom really meant and that it was for us! Sowing seeds into God's kingdom is the best financial investment one can make.

Sowing is something that we all know about. It is a simple process. You plant your seeds into the ground, they come up, and finally, you get to harvest what you have planted. We plant a garden every year. We prepare the soil before we start planting our seeds. Let's say we are planting squash seeds. Now if we plant squash seeds, we know and expect to harvest squash in the near future. Sound simple? It is! The kingdom of God is the same process. We know that if you plant in good, fertile soil, the seeds will come up and do better than if they are planted into any other type of ground. Planting seeds into the kingdom of God should be done just like you would plant your own seeds in a garden or field.

You should do some research on the ground that you are planting in, and make sure it is fertile soil of God and that it is producing fruit for the kingdom of God. You need to plant your seed or tithe your money where you receive your spiritual nourishment from God. You must pray and ask God to direct your planting, though, because this is a vital part of reaping the harvest.

We started planting or tithing into the kingdom of God in 2003. Yes, we had tithed on a regular basis before 2003, but this particular year was different. We starting naming our tithe seed debt freedom. I kept the vision of debt freedom in front of our eyes every day. I wrote out a notecard that said, "We are planting seeds by faith. We believe that our home and all of our bills will be paid in full by the harvest of our seeds!" I placed it on the refrigerator for us to see every day. We spoke and prayed over our seed and harvest every day. We also begin to name our seeds. Each time that I wrote out a tithe check, I wrote on the memo part exactly what the seed was supposed to accomplish. For example, debt freedom or whatever we needed at the time. The more seeds that we planted, the greater the harvest was! We, by the mercy and grace of God, are now debt-free. God's sowing and reaping, God's financial plan will and does work every time. We accomplished this by speaking debt freedom, praying about debt freedom, and tithing our 10 percent and more of our incomes into God's kingdom.

I know this may be difficult to understand, especially when you look at your own financial situation, and all you see is surviving from one paycheck to the next. You ask, "How can I tithe 10 percent when I don't have enough to buy groceries now." I hear your concerns because that is exactly where we were when we stepped out in faith to learn and place into practice God's financial plan. We discovered in the Bible that if we did tithe back into God's kingdom, we would be blessed. Malachi 3:8–10 (NKJV) reads, "Will a man rob God? Yet you have robbed Me in tithes and offerings. You are cursed with a curse, for you have robbed Me ... Bring all your tithes into the storehouse, that there may be food in My house, and try Me now in this, says the Lord of Host. If I will not open for you in the windows of Heaven and pour out for you such a blessing that there will not be room enough to receive it." You can't outgive God!

I don't share this with you to brag, but I share this life's journey experience with you to show you that God's financial plan and investment are far better than what the world has. We have been debt-free for over eleven years now, and we praise God for the blessing. Yes, we still give our 10 percent and above into the kingdom of God. Yes, we still name our seeds and are expecting a different harvest. We are amazed at what God is doing and will be doing in our futures.

Life's Journeys Application

If you have never tithed or sowed seeds into the kingdom of God, let this be your year of experiencing God's overflowing blessings in your life. As you continue to sow your seeds, remember the promise given to us by Jesus: "Give and it shall be given unto you, good measure, pressed down, and shaken together and running over, shall men give into your bosom. For with the same measure that you use, it will be measured back to you" (Luke 6:38 NKJV).

The promise will never fail or be broken. Every time that you sow, the promise is yours. Sow your seeds into God's kingdom with mighty expectations for your situation today and in the future.

****

New Things

> Therefore if anyone is in Christ, he is a new creature: the old things have passed away; behold all things have become new. (2 Corinthians 5:17 NKJV)

The beginning of a new year always provides us with an opportunity to evaluate our lives and the things we have said and done over the previous year. As we look back, we might find that we have been highly blessed and favored in all parts of our lives, or we may only see the many disappointments, heartaches, and goals that were left unaccomplished. Whatever the past year has brought you, there is no time to dwell on what has happened. It's time to look forward. As we stop looking back and begin looking at the new year and a new journey with Jesus, we have an opportunity for a brand-new start.

For those who need salvation, God offers the greatest opportunity to begin a brand-new life. Second Corinthians 5:17 (NKJV) says "if anyone is in Christ, he is a new creature." Even if we are saved, we need to reach out and grab hold of this opportunity to start anew and afresh again.

All of us can be pulled down by our negative attitudes, bad habits, and even the world that we live in. We commit sins in our lives every day, and our flesh will corrupt our thinking if we allow it. We can be surrounded by many spiritual forces, but through Christ, everything changes. "Old things," no matter how corrupt, have "passed away." Everything becomes new! He can forgive all our sins … free us from all guilt, worry, stress … and give us the direction and wisdom that we need.

Life's Journey Application

Today, you can have everything erased. You can leave your burdens behind. You can start over again and become new in Christ. No matter how many years you might have been a Christian, you still can be renewed and allow the old things in your life to pass away.

Ask God to forgive your sins, take away your fears and anxieties, and renew you in body, soul, and spirit. Start living in the newness of life that God has prepared for you in Christ Jesus! My prayer for each of you is that you will commit the past into God's hands. Ask Him to make you a brand-new creature. Praise Him for all He will make new in your life. May each of you find favor, healings, and God's touch in this brand-new journey you are taking with Jesus.

****

Enlarging Our Territories

Now Jabez was more honorable than his brothers, and his mother called his name Jabez, saying that I bore him in pain. And Jabez called on the God of Israel saying, "Oh, that You would bless me indeed, and enlarge my territory, that Your hand would be with me, and that You would keep me from evil, that I may not cause pain!" So God granted him what he requested. (1 Chronicles 4:9–10 NKJV)

What would happen if we as ordinary Christians decided to stretch our spiritual faith and reached out to God with such a prayer to take and transform us to a life of extraordinary, overflowing abundances and radically change our lives and the lives of others for His glory? That's exactly what Jabez did. He stretched his spiritual faith and reached out to God with a prayer. In his short prayer, he asked God to bless him with more territory, more land, more wealth, more favor, more blessings, and protection. God really does have unclaimed blessings waiting for us.

It tells us in Matthew 7:7 (NKJV), "Ask it will be given unto you; seek, and you will find, knock, and it will be opened to you." There is no limit to God's goodness! We must seek Him and ask Him for a blessing and expect our blessings. If we fail to ask Him for our blessings, we will not receive all that God has for us. God's overflowing bounty is limited only by us, not by His unlimited resources, power, or willingness to give. Jabez was blessed simply because he refused to let any obstacle, person, or opinion loom larger than His God. He had faith and believed.

Life's Journey Application

My prayer for each of you is that God will increase your territories. That He may give each of you a new vision and the will and capabilities to grow in your faith. I pray that each of you will be generous with your time, your resources, your talents, and your gifts to reach out to others God places in your path. Share what God has blessed you with. May each of you be courageous to grow and to go wherever God leads you.

Lord, make each of us more aware of the people You have divinely appointed for us to meet. I pray that He makes you ambitious to win lost souls. When you ask, you will receive; when you seek, you will find; when you knock, it will be opened to you!

May God enlarge your personal territory with blessings and favor. May He use each of you to enlarge His Kingdom.

Are You Stuck?

My almost two-year-old grandson has a new saying in his vocabulary: "Papa, I'm stuck." We all know how easy it is for a two-year-old to get stuck in all kinds of places and situations. However, he knows if he gets stuck, someone will be there to set him free! He has innocent trust and pure faith that someone will come to his rescue.

We also have someone to help us when we are stuck in a rut. It is so easy for us to arrive at a place in our spiritual walk with God when we look around and discover we are stuck—not moving forward and not moving backward. Stuck! At these particular times, we are the weakest and the most vulnerable to the Enemy coming into our lives. It is at these times that the Enemy will come in like a flood to kill, steal, and try to destroy us. During these times, we must call out to Jesus! Have childlike faith, and trust that Jesus will help to set us free.

Life's Journey Application

Just like my grandson calls out to be freed from his stuck places and situations, all you have to do is say, "Jesus, I'm stuck." He can and will set you free. He will guide you on His spiritual path.

Arise, take that step, and call out to Jesus! He will lift you out of the miry clay that holds you in the rut.

. . . .

For Everything There Is a Season

The Bible tells us that "To everything there is a season, a time for every purpose under Heaven" (Ecclesiastes 3:1 NKJV). Yes, there is a time to speak and a time to be silent, a time to wait, and a time to act. But how do we know the right time? As most of you know, I have personally been going through a very different and difficult season in my life the last several months. I truly know and believe that God has a divine plan and purpose for this season in my life. I have a very special throw pillow that simply states, "For everything there is a season." We may not enjoy the cold, dark seasons of our lives, but we must keep our eyes on Jesus because there is a divine plan being developed just for us. God demonstrated that He knows the right time for every purpose. He sent Jesus into this world at just the right time. He will also send the perfect preparations into our lives when everything is complete and ready according to His plan. God is still on the throne, reigning on high.

We may have prayed about our troubles and uncertainties, physical or financial problems, or needs on our jobs. We may know people who need God's help. If we haven't received the answers, it can appear that God is not listening or even there for us. We must keep hidden in our hearts the words that say, "I will never leave you or forsake you" (Hebrews 13:5 NKJV). As we walk through the dark seasons of our lives, we must not become impatient (which is easy to do) or give up hope. Instead, we must be persistent, keep obeying Him, keep praying, keep praising Him, keep seeking Him, keep trusting Him, have faith, and believe that He will walk us through the season.

Always remember that God will answer prayers and provide for our needs in His time. Only He knows the right time for the fulfillment of His purposes. We must also remember there is a right time for us to act, too. When God begins to open the door for us, to lead us out of one season of our lives into the next season, we need to stand up and seize the opportunity that He is giving us. Seek to live your life according to the flow of the different seasons of life He's prepared for us.

Life's Journey Application

I pray that whatever season you are walking through that God reigns down His mercy and grace upon you. May He hold each of you in the palm of His hand and be your shelter from the storms. Make sure in this season that you keep your focus on God and not on the problems that are looming before you.

. . . .

Battle of the Mind

My Sunday school class has been studying about the mind being a battlefield. Our minds can become an open area for battle or warfare if we do not keep ourselves alert and awake to the Enemy's attacks. Not one person that is immune from the mind being a target area for him. The Enemy, when given the smallest amount of leverage, will and does fill our minds with nagging thoughts, suspicions, doubts, and fears. He knows our insecurities, our weaknesses, and what we hold most dear to us. John 10:10 (NKJV) tells us that "The thief comes to kill, steal, and destroy." He will attempt to attack our lives in every area that we allow him to. The Enemy plants these little insecurities, and if we allow or choose to think upon them, there is a possibility that these little insecurities will and can grow. The Bible says in Proverbs 23:7 (NKJV), "For as he thinks in his heart, so is he." Our minds are the centers of all our actions. A quote from the *Battlefield of the Mind* by Joyce Meyers says, "Our actions are a direct result of our thoughts. If we have a negative mind, we will have a negative life. We act upon what we think about. It is so very important for each of us to learn how to use God's spiritual warfare against these attacks."

What can us as believers do to counteract these attacks and these spiritual battles? We must first realize that we do not fight against each other. The Word of God says in Ephesians 6:12 (NKJV), "For we do not wrestle against flesh and blood, but against principalities, against powers, against rulers of the darkness of this age, against spiritual host of weaknesses in heavenly places." The Word tells us that our battles are not flesh and blood but spiritual. We can overcome the wiles of the Enemy when we stand tall and firm upon the Word of God! God's Word tells each of us how to be victorious in living.

Life's Journey Application

You can arm yourselves with God's spiritual weapons. Start with the Word of God. Quote the Word in your prayers. Quote the Word out loud when in a battle. Pray and seek God. Develop a closer relationship with your heavenly Father. Praise, praise God from the bottom of your heart even when you do not feel like praising Him. Give your all to God. He will never leave you or forsake you.

I pray that God will reveal Himself and His Word to each of you as you develop a stronger relationship with Him. I encourage each of you to stand strong, do not be afraid, and believe that our God can change any situation.

. . . .

Is Your Plate Full?

Is your plate of life full and overflowing? Is life keeping you on a fast track? Do you have a difficult time shutting down the constant twirling thoughts that go around and around in your mind? If this is you, I want you to know that the Enemy is trying to keep you busy! He is also trying to keep your mind full of all kinds of thoughts, worries, and fears. Why would he do this? The answer is really very simple; he does not want you to spend time in the presence of God. The Enemy works overtime to keep us busy and our minds cluttered. John 10:10 (NKJV) says, "The thief does not come except to steal, and to kill, and to destroy, I have come that they may have life and that they may have it more abundantly." The Enemy tries to steal our time away so we cannot spend it with God. Don't allow him to. Jesus came to give us life and life more abundantly. When our lives are so busy, our minds have hard times shutting off to the things that are going on around us. The Word says in 1 Peter 1:13 (NKJV), "Therefore gird up the loins of our mind." This simply means take control of our thoughts that go constantly in our minds. We need to stay focused on our heavenly Father and all the things that He wants us to do. We must put our blinders on, and focus on the only thing that really matters—our God.

We need to stand still and allow the peace of God to flow over us. Second Chronicles 20:12 (NKJV) reads, "For we have no power against this great multitude that is coming against us; nor do we know what to do, but our eyes are upon You." What an awesome verse. The people had finally realized that they had no might against their enemies. They also did not know what to do. They eventually realized that all they needed was to have their eyes focused on God, and everything would work out according to His plan and His purpose!

Life's Journey Application

We all find ourselves in different walks in our journeys when our lives and plates are overflowing. We must stop and reflect on why our plates are full, and lay down the things that are keeping us so busy at the feet of God; He is more than capable of taking care of it for you. Give your twirling thoughts over to God; He will replace the thoughts with His peace and wisdom. Seek after God in the midst of your overflow!

. . . .

Past Battles Equals New Beginnings

Have you ever looked back at your time hop or calendar to see what you were doing last year or even the year before that? My calendar from the previous year was showing the dates that I was facing a battle and preparing for one of the hardest times in my life's journey.

Each of us will go through some kind of a battle in our life's journey, but we must always remember there is always a victory after the battle. It may not necessarily be the victory that we think we should have, but it will be the victory God wants us to have.

I want to share with you the prayer that I wrote the night before I started my first chemo treatment. I feel some of you need to be reminded that our God is still on the throne. He will take you through whatever you are facing. One of my favorite sayings has always been, "When your back is against the wall, praise the Lord!" I know that when you face darkness, fear, and whatever life throws at you, it is very difficult to praise the Lord, keep a song of praise on your lips, and a song in your heart!!

I want each of you to know that God and only God saw me through that detour in my life's journey. Praises to Him! Just call out to Him. Seek Him. Matthew 11:28 (NKJV)tells us, "Come to Me, all you who labor, and are heavy laden and I will give you rest."

Here is my prayer.

Father, take my hands that I may be able to lift them to pray to you, keep my spirit sealed in Yours. Give my body strength to endure whatever is coming my way. Walk before me through this journey. Help me, Lord, to keep a song of praise upon my lips. I know that I am under the wings of the Almighty. Wrap them around me tightly. I know that I am an anointed child of Yours. I praise You for using this part of my journey to help someone else along the way. I still don't understand, but I know that this is one part of my life's journey that I have no control over. I must lean upon You for Your strength, knowing that all things have a purpose and a plan. I know that this part of my life's journey will somehow glorify You. I know what You bring me to, You will bring me through. I place my full trust, my faith, my cares, my fears, at your holy feet. I give up the control that I think that I must have over to You. You are more than capable to handle this part of my journey! Hide me under your wings! Hold me in the palm of Your Hand.

Father, fill me with Your unspeakable joy and peace and Your perfect peace that passes all understanding. The perfect peace that only You can give. I know that You will never leave me or forsake me. You are right here beside me. When You are not beside me, You are walking ahead of me. I know that I am covered by the precious blood of Jesus. This difficult part of my journey was on the mind of Jesus the day that He was crucified. The day that He died for my sins, my transgressions, and my healings, I was on His mind! I know everything will be all right because I serve a mighty God!

Lord, I know as Your child and Your servant, You will take me over this mountain and walk me through the fire. I will be victorious. I will not be afraid. I will not be fearful. I will praise Your holy name. Amen.

Life's Journey Application

We serve a mighty God. Do not hesitate to call out to Him. Whatever life is throwing at you right now, just know that God can and will see you through. Do not be afraid. Just cast your cares at the feet of Jesus.

****

Directions of Our Thoughts

We serve a great and awesome God! He has created us with complex minds as the control centers of our bodies. It is the control center for everything that happens in the body. One of the things that He gave each of us when He created our minds was freewill over our thoughts. Now, with the freewill that He so gracious gave us, it is up to each of us on how we direct our different thought patterns. The question is, What direction do you allow your thoughts to wander? Our minds do like to wander around. Some more than others! However, we have the choice in the direction that we want our thoughts to go.

God has given each of us the ability to think about things that are pure, lovely, positive, and honorable. However, since we have freewill, the Enemy will also place negative, ugly, sinful, and disrespectable thoughts into our minds.

The Enemy likes to get us thinking about things that will have us looking away from God and all of His glory. He thinks if he can keep our minds occupied on several things, we will get our them off God. We must guard our thoughts! We need to keep our minds on one thing, and that is our Lord Jesus Christ. Then your thoughts will line up with Him.

Life's Journey Application

The next time you find yourself dwelling on negative things, refocus your thoughts on the things that are positive. The way you see life will largely determine what you get out of it. Keep your eyes focused on God. He is the way, the truth, and the Light!

****

In God's Presence

We each need time in our lives to step back from our busy schedules and seek rest and relaxation. Our physical bodies get to a point where they need rest and time to recharge. Each of you probably have a special getaway place that you can go to find that needed rest, relaxation, and most important of all, recharging. Our special place is in eastern Oklahoma, near Broken Bow. The moment we arrive at the cabin, you can actually feel the peace and tranquility start to surround you. The awesome beauty of God's presence and His majestic touch can be seen in the small running creek, tall pines, the quietness of the evenings, the breathtaking views, the gorgeous fall leaves, the freshness of the air, and the towering mountains. In the presence of God's beauty, we find much-needed rest, and our physical batteries begin to recharge.

But what about when our spiritual batteries need to be recharged? We must retreat into His presence! In the presence of God, you will experience rest and peace. He will surround you with His peace. In His presence, all that you experience will begin to feel and look different.

The very moment that you step into His presence, you will feel your spiritual batteries start their recharging.

All things, all problems, all schedules seem to vanish when you are in His presence.

Life's Journey Application

Take time to rest, relax, and recharge your physical batteries. Step away from your busy schedules, and plug into a few days of pure fun and relaxation. But remember that even more important than recharging your physical bodies is to make sure your spiritual batteries are recharged. Plug into the power of God!

****

Forgiveness

> Take heed to yourselves. If your brother sins against you, rebuke him; and if he repents, forgive him. And if he sins against you seven times in a day, and seven times in a day returns to you, saying, "I repent," you shall forgive him. (Luke 17:3–4 NKJV)

Now we don't mind the rebuking part of these verses. We can rebuke all day. In fact, it comes quite naturally. But when Jesus said to rebuke, it wasn't a license for us to act mean or behave in a nasty way or treat others with a bad attitude. In other words, when someone offends us, we really want to tell them off. Our flesh wants to act and to act fast, but that's not what Jesus was talking about. He was telling us to be careful and to do it in love, always seeking the good of the other person. Easy to say, but much harder to do. But we can, and we must!

We don't mind the repentance part as long as it's somebody else who is doing it. If someone offends us and then comes back and apologizes, we can often or should be able to just go ahead and let it go. But come on, Jesus said seven times in one day. Wow! How much of this treatment are we supposed to take? Jesus said, "You shall forgive him." Turn the other cheek, and turn it again, as many times as needed. Well, it's one thing when they offend us and then they repent, and we forgive them. What about when they don't repent? Are we still supposed to forgive them? Yes!

We don't forgive other people because they need it. We forgive them because *we* need it. Forgiveness is the key that unlocks the door to our freedom. Freedom from all the unhealthy side effects of the past hurts in our lives. When we hold onto unforgiveness toward other people, we aren't hurting them, we are hurting ourselves.

We forgive people, not for their sake, but for ours. Your unforgiveness may not even affect them, but it will certainly affect you. Until you forgive a person who has wronged you, you allow him or her to control you.

But what if they aren't sorry? They don't have to be sorry in order for you to forgive them. Forgiveness is the deliberate choice to release a person from all obligations he or she has toward us as a result of any offense the individual committed against us. There is nothing in that definition that requires action on the part of the guilty party.

There is no doubt about it, forgiveness is extremely difficult. We human beings are very carnal and imperfect. We are at times very quick to become angry, quick to blame others, slow to forgive, and even slower to forget! God forgives and forgets instantly. But we tend to hold on to the grudges, and most of the time, we keep the grudge in the back of our minds until we need to pull it out to be used against that person.

Yet, as Christians, we are commanded to forgive others, just as we, too, have been forgiven. We need all the strength we can absorb from God in order to love and forgive. We need the power of prayer and the power of His compassion within us.

Forgiveness is a conscious choice that you make. It is an act of the will, not the emotions. Forgiveness is the way that God gives you to be freed from the past, to be freed from those who have hurt you. To refuse to forgive is to stay in a prison that will keep you from ever enjoying the full abundance of life that Jesus wants you to have.

There are three steps on the way to forgiveness.

1. Face the pain.

2. Release the pain of the offense to God.

3. Be able to approach the offender with love.

Life's Journey Application

Are you experiencing unforgiveness in your life? Do you need to forgive so that you can move forward? I urge you to take this message, and apply it to those areas of your life that you need to forgive and to the people you need to forgive.

Forgiveness is a choice, and you must make that choice. Don't allow the Enemy to bring you back into the slavery of unforgiveness. Through forgiveness you shall be set free. So enjoy your freedom! "Therefore, If the Son makes you free, you shall be free indeed" (John 8:36 NKJV).

Believe, Begin, Become

Do you have the power of three? One must believe, then begin, and then become all that you can be. To me, I immediately think about the power of the mighty three—God, Jesus, and the Holy Spirit. When you have the power of the three, you can believe, begin, and become all that God has intended you to be.

The power of the three!

Believe

1. You must believe. You must believe in yourself. The first step to do this is to start forgiving yourself. Ask God to help you get rid of all the unforgiveness and sin in your life. Believe that He can do all things. He can make you a new person in Christ Jesus.

2. You must believe in and have an expectation for your life. Take a step forward, put your trust and faith in Jesus, and start expecting the favor of God in your life. Seek Him. He will tell you about and guide you on the right direction for your life. Afterward, set that expectation goal high because you can do all things through Jesus Christ who strengthens you!

3. You must believe and place God as your top priority. Develop a close walk with Him. He will never leave you or forsake you.

Start this very moment. Start believing that you are a child of the Most High God. Start believing that you can. Start believing. There is power whenever someone shows up and starts believing!

Begin

1. You must begin. You do not have time to sit still; you must get up and get going! I feel deeply that God wants me to arise. Start today with what you have been putting off. You know, those things that have been a dream and an expectation all your life. Don't wait. If you can believe it, you must make a step forward and begin. Ask God to open the doors that have been closed to your dream. I know for a fact that what God opens, no one can close. So what are you waiting on?

2. You must begin to show more of Jesus in your life. The way that you do this is to start a relationship with Him, begin reading your Bible, start attending church, and start praying (or as some say, just talking to God). People will begin to see a different you.

3. Beginnings must start somewhere. So believe that you can and then begin on your journey.

Become

I pray that you become all that God wants you to be! There is power in the threes—God-Jesus-Holy Spirit; believe-begin-become. There is a Bible character who did the power of the threes. His name was David. You all know the story of David and Goliath. David believed that he could defeat Goliath. Why did he believe that? Because he had a relationship with God! He had witnessed the power of God in his life. David had to take a step or begin the walk toward the giant. He had to begin. Everything has a starting point, and this was one of David's starting points. When he experienced victory over the giant, it started him on the road to become all that God had ordained for him to do.

Life's Journey Application

How can you start believing in the power of the threes? How can you place this believe, begin, and become in your life's journey? Make a point this day to start on this life-changing part of your journey. Remember, it is one step at a time.

. . . .

God Is My Shield

A shield has many definitions according to *Webster's Dictionary:* to protect, to cover, and to conceal, to shelter, armor, defense, to guard, and a buffer. The origin of the word "shield" comes from the Hebrew language. Its meaning in the Hebrew language is "to defend" and "the protective guard of God." The shield is a common biblical symbol for protection and is a very important part of the armor of God.

> Finally, my brethren, be strong in the Lord and in the power of His might. Put on the whole armor of God that you may be able to stand against the wiles of the devil. For we do not wrestle against flesh and blood, but against principalities, against powers, against the rulers of the darkness of this age, against spiritual hosts of wickedness in the heavenly places. Therefore, take up the whole armor of God that you may be able to stand in the evil day, and having done all to stand. Stand therefore, having girded your waist with truths, having put on the breastplate of righteousness, And having shod your feet with the preparation of the gospel of peace; Above all, taking the shield of faith with which you will be able to quench all the fiery darts of the wicked one. And take the helmet of salvation, and

the sword of the Spirit, which is the Word of God. (Ephesians 6:10–17 NKJV)

Look at verse 16, "Above all." "Above all" means the shield is to be used against everything, and the shield is to cover the whole armor. The Christian's shield offers protection against all the fiery darts of the Wicked One. Flaming arrows could not penetrate the fireproof shield of the ancient Roman soldier. Nor can Satan's assaults penetrate to the believers who places their faith in God.

Take up that shield of faith! The battles of life require the shield of God.

David spoke these words to the Lord on the day that God delivered him from his enemies.

> The Lord is my rock and my fortress and my deliver. The God of my strength, in whom I will trust. My shield and the horn of my salvation. My stronghold and my refuge. My Savior, You saved me from violence. I will call upon the Lord who is worthy to be praised. So shall I be saved from my enemies. (2 Samuel 22:2–4 NKJV)

David knew exactly who shielded him during the time of his battle. We must know beyond a shadow of a doubt that God is our shield. God is our shield before the battle, during the battle, and after the battle. I know that God is my shield, but He gently reminded me of His powerful shield of protection on a dark and snowy morning.

First, I want to give God all the glory and the praise for placing His shield of protection around me. I left Duncan about 5:45 a.m., dark and rainy (the Enemy likes to keep you in the dark if you allow him) to drive to Maysville to pick up my younger sister up. She had an appointment in Oklahoma City at nine. I got into the worst snowstorm that I have ever experienced around the Elmore City area. The flakes were coming down so hard and heavy that I was even unsure if I was on the road or not. (It may even appear to you the Enemy wants you to stop, that you can't do this, or just to turn around.) But I was sure if I stopped, someone would hit me. Besides, I couldn't tell where I was because of the heavy snow that was falling. I couldn't see a clear foot in front of my car. The Enemy tried to paralyze me with fear. (He will always try to get you to give up right before your miracle or your victory.) My heart was beating so loudly, I could hear it in my ears. I actually felt at times that my car was sitting still, and I was inside a snow globe. (The Enemy will try to make you lose your place in Christ by blinding you to the truth. He will attempt to shake your world upside down; don't let him.) My fingers gripped the steering wheel until I thought I would have blisters. (Hold on tight to God when you go through the battles.) The snow was piling up on the windshield so fast that my wipers could not keep up; I had to scrunch down in the seat to look through the windshield. Through it all, I just kept praying. Then suddenly I heard this still, small voice deep inside me say, *I am your shield and will walk before you.* I knew in my spirit that all was well, but in my natural eyes, it looked impossible.

Praise God, I did finally make it to Maysville about the breaking of dawn. (There is a light at the end, so keep moving forward.) All I could do after I got there was to praise God for safely bringing me through the horrible storm. However, it was not over. We still had to be in Oklahoma City by nine, so we prayed and once again got back on the snowy and slick road. We got as far as Purcell, and the traffic on I35 was just crawling and the road was in horrible condition. As we sat at the truck stop, I prayed, and we made the decision to return home. I thought we were free and clear driving back on the same road that we had just came down, but when you least expect it, the Enemy will come in like a flood. As we left Purcell, headed back home, I almost lost control of the car. I fishtailed all over my side of the road and barely missed traffic coming toward us. My sister wanted me to pull over so that she could drive. I told her no. That would have let fear defeat me. Besides, I knew that God was with us!

Now I know that there was a reason for this delay and a reason for me driving in the dark, the rain, the blinding snow, and slick roads because God has His perfect timing and reasoning for all things. I will see and understand someday.

When I finally made it safely home, I noticed the Bible verse that I had read right before I left that morning. "Blessed are those who trust in the Lord and have made the Lord their hope and confidence" (Jeremiah 17:7 NIT). God was and is my shield!

Life's Journey Application

Have you ever been in a situation where fear was gripping you? Think back to that experience and know that God brought you through it by being your shield. If you're going through a current situation that has caused fear to loom up within you, stop and know that God is your shield for safety and protection.

****

Spiritual Checkup

It's time for each of us to take a personal spiritual inventory of our lives. You go to the doctor for a physical checkup, the dentist for a cleaning and a checkup, and you even take your car to be checked over. So why not take a little time to give your spirit a checkup.

How do you do this? Please read these questions below and seriously ask yourself and God if your spirit is empty, half full, or full and running over. If you see some area where you are falling short, pray and ask God to fill you up!

1. Have you read your Bible today? Have you read it in the last week? Have you read it in the last month? Do you have to locate your Bible when you go to church? Does it have dust on it from sitting on your end table? If you could not honestly answer these questions, your spirit may need a tune-up.

2. When was the last time you prayed? Was it only when you were faced with a problem? Have you prayed for others? Have you taken the time to enter into a conversation with Jesus? Do you just give Him a list of wants when you pray? If you are having trouble answering these questions about your prayer life, you might need to have a spiritual tune-up.

3. When was the last time you went to church? Do you go just out of habit? Do you just go on Sunday morning and believe that just being in church will keep you spiritually fed until the next Sunday morning? Do you go to seek the face of God Almighty? Do you listen to the message from the pastor, or do you rehearse in your mind all of the things you need to do? Just because you attend church does not mean that you will get a place in heaven. Ask God to give you a spiritual checkup in your attitudes about attending church.

4. When was the last time that you actually lifted your hands into the air and gave God praise? Was it at church last week, last month? Do you sing His praises in your home, on your job, or in your car? Praising God is so important. If you are not

praising Him with your whole heart, soul, and spirit, it is time for a praise checkup.

5. When was the last time that you asked God for guidance in your life? You ask your husband, your wife, your family, your friends, your coworkers, your Facebook friends, your pastor, and your church family, but do you ask the One who knows the exact plan and purpose for you? When was the last time you followed exactly what He told you to do? If you are not asking God for His will and plan in your life, it is time for a spiritual checkup.

6. When was the last time that you turned off your TV, turned off your laptop, turned off your cell phone, crawled into your secret private place with God, and spent some time with Him? We are too busy with all of our technology to give God even a passing glance of our time. If you see yourself in this technology overload, unplug and plug into the presence of God Almighty!

7. When was the last time that you talked with your children or your grandchildren about Jesus? Do you tell them what God has done for you or what you are expecting God to do? Teach them, read the Word to them, explain to them, pray with them. If you don't, the world will certainly tell them about the evil things of this world. Is it time for a spiritual checkup in your relationship with your children and grandchildren?

8. When was the last time that you blessed someone? Can you recall a certain place, a certain time, a certain person you reached out to and blessed? Are you so self-centered that it is all about you? Do you place the needs of others before your own? Do you have compassion for those going through a tough time? Are you showing the world that you are a child of God? If you cannot remember the last time that you extended a hand

in blessing someone, please pray that God will decrease you and increase Him in your life.

9. When was the last time you forgave someone? Have you forgiven that person or persons who mistreated you or spoke ill of you? When was the last time that you prayed for those who have done you wrong? If you have unforgiveness in your heart, please take some time and ask for forgiveness.

10. When was the last time that you tithed into your church? Tithing is an important part, and if you are not tithing, please seek God and ask Him what you need to do. God only requires 10 percent of what we make, and He blesses you with the other 90 percent.

11. When was the last time you witnessed to someone? Have you ever witnessed to someone? Do you ask God to set those in your path each day who need to hear about salvation? Can you lead someone in the sinner's prayer? Have you prayed the sinner's prayer yourself? If you can't answer yes to any of the above questions, it is time for a spiritual checkup.

Life's Journeys Application

Reread the above questions, and write down the answers to each question. Make sure that you are answering each question as truthfully as possible. If you discover some area in your life that needs a spiritual checkup, focusing on building that area to strengthen your spirit. Keep your spiritual health.

****

Vivid Imagination or Truth

God brought back to my memory a beautiful story my now nine-year-old grandson told me when he was only three years old. Please take into consideration that this little boy has always had a wild and vivid imagination, but this story from a three-year-old was in such detail, almost a firsthand experience. I will always hold this story close to my heart no matter if it was a made-up story from a little boy or a true, firsthand experience.

His story begins with him as a baby, awaiting his departure from heaven to meet his parents for the first time. He told me in detail that there were two different rooms separated by a half-wall. In one of the rooms were all the babies waiting for their first encounter with their parents. He described the room as full of all kinds of babies. The other room was full of babies who were returning from their parents on earth to their places in heaven. He said, "The babies in the departure room [ones headed to be with their parents] could see the babies in the arrival room [heaven], but they could not talk with them."

He said that he can remember the day his name, "Parker Boyles," was called and it was time for him to go meet his parents! He departed at that time from heaven to meet his earthly parents.

I love this story! My mind goes to the words that God spoke to the prophet Jeremiah in Jeremiah 1:5 (NKJV), "Before I formed you in the womb, I knew you. Before you were born, I sanctified you." God knew him, and He knows each one of us.

I want to close out this awesome story with Psalm 139:13–16 (NKJV)

> For You formed my inward parts; You covered me in my mother's womb. I will praise You, for I am fearfully and wonderfully

made; Marvelous are Your works, and that my soul knows very well. My frame was not hidden from You, when I was made in secret, and skillfully wrought in the lowest parts of the earth. Your eyes saw my substance, being yet unformed. And in Your book, they all were written, the days fashioned for me. When as yet there were none of them.

God knows every detail about our lives!

Life's Journey Application

No matter what others have said about you or how you feel about yourself, just know that God formed you just the way He intended. You are a child of God. He loves you for just who and what you are. He has formed and fashioned each of your days, so rejoice and be glad for who you are in Christ Jesus.

****

Self-Evaluation for Chapter 3, New Beginnings

1. How have these messages on new beginnings in life's journey touched your life?

2. Identify one area of your life that you can focus on to overcome and experience new beginnings.

3. After reading "New Beginnings," has your life's journey changed in any way?

****

Notes for Chapter 3

****

CHAPTER 4

SALVATIONS

This is my husband Tom's personnel testimony on how great our God really is to His children.

It says in Revelation 12:11 (NKJV). "And they overcame him, by the Blood of the Lamb and by the word of their testimony."

For some reason, he thought before you went to church you needed to be cleaned up from the worldly sins and filth. He didn't really understand that the blood of Jesus would wash all your sins and worldly living away, never to return again. These thoughts kept him from a true relationship with Jesus for a long time. He didn't feel right about going to church because of his drinking habit. He drank for several years. He didn't think that he could quit.

Finally, there came a day when he felt a strong pull on his heart to start attending church with me. At that time in his life, he didn't really understand why he had such an urgent desire to go to church. I had been praying and seeking God for his salvation and his freedom from the bondage of alcohol for a long time. God only works in His time frame, not in ours. He attended church for about one year, still drinking, but learning that God still loved him and that He sent His only Son to die for him. Tom learned that God would take away the desire for the taste of alcohol if he just asked Him. Tom felt His convictions on his heart to stop drinking. He simply asked Him to help him to stop the drinking. The Word says in John 14:14 (NKJV). "If you ask anything in My name, I will do it." It was done. He was finally freed from long years of drinking alcohol. He is now alcohol-free. Glory to God!

Life's Journey Application

We all have habits we need delivered from. Habits that have kept us wrapped in the chains of bondage. Ask God for His help. My husband stepped out and believed in faith that God was more than able to deliver him from his lifelong habit, and He can do it for you, too. God hears our cries for help. Tom is now an overcomer by the blood of the Lamb and the word of his testimony.

Step into God's presence. Get closer to Him. No matter what you have done or are doing, God will forgive you, deliver you, and mold you for His glory.

****

God Loves You!

For God so loved the world that He gave His only begotten Son that whoever believes in Him, should not perish but have everlasting life. (John 3:16 NKJV)

How much does our God love us? We only need to look toward the cross to answer that question. God's love for us is so great He sent His only Son to this earth to die for our sins and to offer us the precious gift of eternal life. Just imagine that day so long ago when our Jesus was hanging on the cross, battered, bleeding, and dying for our sins. Now think about what was going through His mind before He took that last earthly breath. Now think about Him taking all our sins and sicknesses upon Himself that day. What an awesome love to know that each of us was crossing the mind of our Jesus that day on Calvary. We were on His mind. We were in His heart!

We must decide whether to accept God's precious gift. We have two choices. We can accept Him, or we can reject Him. Have you ever wondered why there were three crosses on Calvary that day? The main cross, the center cross, held our Jesus, the very center of our hearts. The other two crosses held one criminal who accepted Jesus, and the other criminal rejected Him. So we have a choice. Will we ignore it, or will we embrace it? Will we invite Christ to dwell in our hearts and be our all in all, or will we reject the precious gift of our Savior. The decision is ours, and so are the consequences. We must choose wisely and choose today.

Life's Journey Application

The Scripture that everyone has either heard or memorized since they were small children can be found in the book of John, John 3:16 (NKJV0. In this Scripture, Jesus tells each of us about the most wonderful and everlasting love that has ever been or will ever be. A love, that is so wonderful. His everlasting love is so full of mercy and just simple forgiveness. His love is so precious, so rare, and so full of hope, and it can belong to each of us. All we need to do is ask Him for His precious gift. If you do not know Jesus as your Lord and Savior, ask Him to come into your heart today. If you have known Jesus for a while, renew your relationship with Him today.

. . . .

His Strength

> The Lord is my light and my salvation; whom shall I fear?
> The Lord is the strength of my life; of whom shall I be afraid?
> (Psalm 27:1 NKJV)

Have you made God the very center of your life, or is He allowed only a few hours on Sunday morning? Have you genuinely allowed God to reign over every part of your heart and life, or have you attempted to place Him in a small spiritual compartment? Do you just call on Him when you are in a time of need? The answers to these questions will determine the direction of your day and will definitely set the course of your life! God loves each of us so very much. In our times of trouble, He will comfort us; in times of sorrow, He will dry our tears. When we are weak or sorrowful, God is as near as your very next breath. He stands at the door of our hearts and just waits. Make the time to welcome Him in, and allow Him to rule not only your heart but your life. And then accept the peace, the strength, the protection, and the abundance that only God can give.

God's love never changes. He has promised to give us the strength to meet any challenge. God has promised to lift us up and to guide our steps if we will let Him. God has promised us that when we entrust our lives to Him completely, He will give us the courage to face any trial and the wisdom to live in His righteousness. God's hands uplifts those who turn their hearts and prayers to Him. Will we accept God's peace? If we do, we can know that we have been forever touched by the loving, unfailing, and uplifting hand of God.

Life's Journey Application

Here is my prayer for each of you.

Dear Lord, let us turn to You for strength. When we are weak, You lift us up. When our spirits are crushed, You comfort us. When we are victorious, Your Word reminds each of us to be humble. Today and every day, we will turn to You, Father, for strength, for hope, for wisdom, and for salvation. Amen.

****

Spiritual Shopping

I heard a really interesting story about a man who went shopping at a new store across the street from his home. He went shopping to pick up a few items and ended up with a whole basket full. This sounds familiar to all of us. He had no way to carry all of his newly acquired stuff home, so he asked if he could just push the cart home and return it later. His wife discovered him in his kitchen with the store cart, unloading his merchandise. He asked his wife if she would push the cart back to the store. Not sure who returned the cart!

I tell you this story to remind you that even our spiritual cabinets become empty at times. We must go to the spiritual store to be replenished. We need to restore and restock on a daily basis. How do we do this? We simply can't go to the local store with our list of needs and check them off when we have selected them from the store's shelves. We can, however, go to God's shelves. We can find everything that we are in need of for our lives on His shelves.

Life's Journey Application

What is on your spiritual list? Do you need salvation, joy, peace, happiness, financial breakthrough, relationships mended, or healing? Your list can go on and on.

Philippines 4:19 (NKJV) says, "And my God shall supply all your needs according to His riches in glory by Christ Jesus." Go to the His shelves. Spend time looking around in His Holy Word. Try on His armor, and hold up His shield. Look at all He has available just for you. You will be a different person when you have spent time looking and exploring His shelves.

You, too, can come out with a whole shopping cart full of just what you need! Guess what; you don't even have to return the shopping cart!

. . . .

Heaven-Bound

Do not let your heart be troubled; believe in God, believe also in Me. In My Father's House are many dwelling places if it was not so, I would have told you. For I go to prepare a place for you. If I go and prepare a place for you, I will come again and receive you to Myself, that where I am, there you may be also. (John 14:1–3 NASB)

There comes a time in everyone's life when Jesus reaches out His hands and tells you it's time to come home. It is time to come live with Him in the many mansions that He has prepared for us. My family experienced the loss of our dear mother. Yes, it was difficult, and yes, it is still difficult. But I know where my mom is. She is dancing around the throne and singing praises to Jesus. Death is always so hard and appears to be so final, but we as Christians know that life here on this earth is like a blink of the eye compared to eternal life in heaven. We can have peace and hope knowing our loved one stepped into the very presence of Jesus and will live there forever and forever. We know this isn't good-bye but we'll see you later!

How do we know this? Jesus answered that question in His teaching the night He was betrayed. He knew that we would have problems, tribulations, and sorrow in this life, but He said, "We must not let our hearts be troubled" (John 14:1 NKJV). Instead, we should believe in Him, have faith in His Word, and trust Him to provide for us, both in the present and the future. As our thoughts focus on heaven, we realize that He hasn't forgotten us. Rather, He has prepared a glorious place for us. We should think about heaven as our Father's house, filled with "Many dwelling places." Jesus has promised to come for us, so we can be with Him forever. Hallelujah!

Life's Journey Application

You and I may be prepared to meet Jesus, but how about our friends, our loved ones, our coworkers, the person that sits beside you at church, your neighbors, and all the different people we come into contact with on an everyday basis? Do they know how to get to heaven? Do they know Jesus as their personal Lord and Savior? We as Christians, according to Matthew 28:19 (NKJV), "Go therefore and make disciples of all the nations, baptizing them in the name of the Father, and of the Son, and of the Holy Spirit." We have been commissioned to spread the gospel to the entire world. What are we waiting for?

I pray each of us will be empowered by the Holy Spirit to spread the gospel to all we come into contact with. May God bless each of you, and may His grace and mercy fall upon you and your households.

Jesus Christ Can Offer You a New Life!

Are you searching for true happiness? Has your life become meaningless? Have things turned out much differently than you thought they would? Perhaps you have lost your job or someone in your family. Or maybe you just feel empty inside. Maybe you have become addicted to alcohol, gambling, or drugs in the search for happiness. You may have lost your ambition or even your faith in other people. You may feel there is nothing left in life and nowhere to turn. Read these words and find the answers on how to get a new life.

Jesus Christ can offer you a new life. Jesus Christ is a life-changing experience. Jesus Christ can completely change your life and fill it with peace, joy, and happiness. Jesus said, "Come to Me, all you who labor and are heavy laden, and I will give you rest" (Matthew 11:28 NKJV).

The world has become a very selfish, cold place to live. At times it can seem very hard to bear. Jesus is your answer for a new life, for a new future, and for a reason to continue with your life. Let Jesus become your life-changing experience. Once you turn to Jesus, you will not want to return to your old way of life.

You may think you've done so many things wrong that nothing can repair your life. There is hope for you; Jesus will not turn away even the worst sinner. Read the words of Jesus and find the wonderful truths that can give you a new life.

All have sinned.

> For all have sinned, and fall short of the glory of God. (Romans 3:23 NKJV)

God hates sin, but He loves the sinner.

> For God so loved the world that He gave His only begotten Son, that whosoever believes in Him shall not perish, but have everlasting life. (John 3:16 NKJV)

God wants all men to be saved.

> For this is good and acceptable in the sight of God our Savior; who desires all men saved, and to come to the knowledge of the truth. (1 Timothy 2:3–4 NKJV)

Jesus died for our sins, so we could be free.

> For the Son of Man has come to seek and to save that which was lost. (Luke 19:10 NKJV)

Jesus arose from the dead and has the power to save us.

> For the wages of sin is death, but the gift of God is eternal life through Christ Jesus our Lord. (Romans 6:23 NKJV)

He will save the very worst sinner.

> For whosoever calls upon the Name of the Lord shall be saved. (Romans 10:13 NKJV)

We receive Him into our hearts by faith.

> For by grace you have been saved through faith, and that not of yourselves, it is a gift of God. (Ephesians 2:8 NKJV)

A new life is opened up for you.

> Therefore if anyone is in Christ, he is a new creation, old things have passed away, behold, all things have become new. (2 Corinthians 5:17 NKJV)

Only Jesus can save you.

> Nor is there salvation in any other, for there is no other name under heaven given among men, by which we must be saved. (Acts 4:12 NKJV)

Sinners' Prayer

> Lord, forgive me of my sins. Come into my heart. I believe Jesus died for me on the cross and arose again from the dead and is alive forevermore. I receive you now Jesus by faith into my life as my Lord and Savior. By Your grace and power, I will live for you the rest of my life.

Will It Last? That Depends on You

> Being confident of this very thing, that He who has begun a good work in you will complete it until the day of Jesus Christ. (Philippians 1:6 NKJV)

Life's Journey Application

What Is the Next Step?

Now that you have given your heart and life to Jesus, you will want to attend church regularly. You will want to fully experience this life-altering experience. I believe that you need to read the Bible. Place the Words deep within you. Start living your life for Jesus.

Always remember that God's Word is the final authority, and it has the answers to every question and problem that we may face. God will lead and direct you. You will now have peace and assurance that you have a new life, and you will go on to live forever with Jesus when you die. You can know for sure in your heart that your future is sealed, and you will live in heaven.

If you are already living for Jesus, please share this article with your lost loved ones, lost friends, and lost coworkers. We must be about our Father's business!

. . . .

A Life Turnaround

Sometimes people think they are too old to change their ways of living. I strongly disagree with this statement. I serve a mighty, living, and all-powerful God who can and will change people's lives no matter how old they are or how young they are. Nothing, I say nothing, is too hard for our God.

I was reminded of the story of the Samaritan woman immediately after my conversation with this person. She, too, thought that after all she had been through in her life of sin, things would never change for her. That is exactly what happened until the day that she went to draw water at the well and had a Jesus encounter. Just a few moments in the presence of Jesus changed this woman forever. It can change you, too.

This woman was going about her daily life one day, when she went to the well to draw water in her water pot. I believe that she went in the late afternoon to avoid being around others, others who ridiculed and degraded her because of the sin in her life. Be very careful how you look at and judge other people. I believe that she was astonished to see a Jewish man, standing by the well, and I believe that she was probably speechless when He asked her for a drink of water. You see, Jews did not talk with the Samaritan people. It was just something they did not do. She didn't know it, but she was standing in the presence of Jesus. They proceeded to talk, and Jesus began telling her about all the husbands that she had and the one that she was living with now. God knows your every secrets. He knows your every sin. Nothing hidden from Him.

I believe at this point she knew deep down in her spirit that she was in the presence of God Almighty. She was so excited she left her water pot at the well to run back to the village to tell everyone about this Man she just met and talked with. The leaving of her water pot at the well can be translated to leaving her old life behind and emerging out of it as a new creation in Christ. Old things were gone, and all things became new.

This woman at the well had spent a lifetime looking for the right man but had never found him. At the well that afternoon, just outside of Samaria, the right Man found her and changed her life forever. Jesus will always find you regardless of where you are or what you have done.

Life's Journey Application

I pray this day that whatever has happened in your life to make you feel like you are too old to have a turnaround, is broken by the power of the blood of Jesus. I pray that the same Jesus who met with the Samaritan woman meets with you today. I pray that you will leave your water pot (whatever is holding you back from living a life with God) at the feet of Jesus today. May God richly bless you and keep you in His presence.

. . . .

Letter of Salvation

I have been carrying a heavy burden deep down in my spirit for my family and friends. I needed to make sure all of my family and friends knew about Jesus and accepted Him as their Savior. So, to make sure that this heavy burden left me, I wrote this letter to give each of them. I know that many of you are saved, but there are several who are not. Even if you are saved, we must daily work out our own salvation with fear and trembling, and for those who do not know Jesus, now is the time.

Dear family and friends,

Jesus loves you! He wants you to have total victory in every area of your life. He wants you to be free. Free from your past and all the things that hold you back from fulfilling your purpose in life and achieving your dreams and goals. Jesus wants you! God knows all about you. He knows the mistakes you have made in your life. He knows the hurt, pain, and disappointments you have gone through and maybe caused others. Jesus wants to free you from the pain, the hurts, and the memories that haunt you. Let Jesus set you free, free from the prison of your past and your future, by asking Him into your life as your Lord and Savior and allowing Him to become Lord of all of your life. By doing this you will have a life of love, joy, peace, victory, success, freedom, but more important than all of these is eternity with Jesus!

God said in His Word Romans 10:13 (NKJV), "For Whosoever calls on the name of the Lord shall be saved. In the book of Romans 10:9 (NKJV), "That if you confess with your mouth the Lord Jesus, and believe in your heart that God raised Him from the dead, you will be saved. For with the heart man believes unto righteousness; and with the mouth confession is made unto salvation" (Romans 10:9, 10—13).

Life's Journey Application

Just say this prayer.

Dear heavenly Father,

I confess with my mouth and believe in my heart that Jesus Christ is the Son of God. I believe that God raised Jesus from the dead. God, I am sorry for all the wrong I have done. Please forgive me. I repent (I turn from anything that is not pleasing to You). Jesus, I am calling upon You to save me right now! Jesus, come live in my heart, and be my Savior and Lord of my life. Make me the person You intended for me to be. Make every desire line up with Your purpose. God, I thank you in Jesus's name for saving me, forgiving me, cleansing me with Your blood. Amen.

If you prayed this prayer, then welcome to the family of God. The angels in heaven are rejoicing at this very moment because of you and what you have just done. I will be praying that you will allow God to lead you to a local church that teaches and preaches the Word of God.

I will be praying that each of you share this letter with your family and your friends!

****

Chapter 4 – Self–Evaluations

1. Have you accepted Jesus as your Lord and Savior? It's simple; just ask Jesus to forgive you of your sins and confess with your mouth that you want Jesus to come into your heart.

2. After reading the different salvation and deliverance messages, how has your life's journey been changed?

3. If you have been saved for a while, how have these messages strengthened your walk with Jesus?

****

Notes for Chapter 4

****

CHAPTER 5

THE KING IS COMING

Who rules in your life?

> You shall have no other gods before Me. (Exodus 20:3 NKJV)

I have to tell each of you about a wonderful experience that happened while I was watching my two three-year-old grandchildren. One of my favorite things to do when I am babysitting them is to watch and listen to them talk and play together. This peculiar day, I had noticed that they had gone into my bedroom, so I went and stood in the doorway and witnessed them talking and touching my Jesus statue. This peculiar Jesus statue is about two feet tall and has very lifelike features. The statue has the crown of thorns on His head, blood drops on His face and shoulders, and clear drops of tears running down His cheeks. Parker asked, "Why is Jesus crying?" Jadyn replied, "Because people do not go to church." I stood there, listening to this innocent three-year-old conversation, when I suddenly realized how true that little statement was. People place other things in their lives above God. God is not their top priority in life. They have no time for Him in their lives.

Now I will ask each of you some questions. Who rules your heart? Is it God, or is it something else? Do you give God your firstfruits or your last? Have you given Jesus your heart, your soul, your talents, and your life, or have you given Him little more than a few hours each Sunday morning? Have you talked about or thought about who rules your heart? Now is the time to take the advice of childlike faith, dig deep into your hearts, and make sure that Jesus is your Lord and Savior.

In the book of Exodus, God warns that we should place no gods before Him. Yet all too often, we place our God in second, third, or fourth place as we worship the gods of pride, greed, work, sports, power, or things that we do for entertainment. Sometimes we worship other gods without even realizing what we are doing. We tend to make time for the things that are important to us. But as I think about the childlike faith question and answer, I want to make sure that God is top priority in my life and in the lives of those around me. What could be more important that your salvation and your eternal life with Jesus?

Does God rule your heart? Take a moment and ask yourself this question. If your answer is no, please ask Jesus to forgive you, and seek Him as the only ruler of your heart. Make certain that the honest answer to this question is a yes. In the life of every believer, God comes first, and that's precisely the right place that He deserves in your heart.

Do not continue to put off your salvation because Jesus is coming soon to take His children home. You do not want to be left behind.

Life's Journey Application

I pray this prayer for each of you.

Dear Lord, help each of us to have no other gods before You. Show us, Lord, what we have placed higher than our relationship with You. Help us to have a closer relationship with You. Lord, in every part of our lives, let us place You first. Let our words and actions honor You, and let our relationship with others be a reflection of the love You have for us. You sent Your Son Jesus to die on the cross for us. Jesus had to endure so much suffering and then death so that we might live. Because He lives, we, too, have Your promise of eternal life. Help us, God, to place You above all things in our lives. Help us, Lord, to be ready when the trumpet blows, signaling the return of Your Son.

. . . .

Are You Ready?

But of that day and hour no one knows, not even the angels of heaven, but My Father only. But as the days of Noah were, so also will the coming of the Son of Man be. For as in the days before the flood, they were eating and drinking, marrying and giving in marriage, until the day that Noah entered the ark and did not know until the flood came and took them all away, so also will the coming of the Son of Man be. (Matthew 24:36–39 NKJV)

I am sure you have heard the rapture was supposed to have occurred on several specific days in the past, but those predictions never came to pass. Why? The Bible tells us very plainly that no one knows the day or the time when Jesus comes back to get His children.

As each day that was predicted came and went, I started thinking about the real day when Jesus steps out and we, as His children, rise up to meet Him in the air. I started asking myself, "Are you ready for that day?" I have started living each day as if it could be that day. So I ask you, "Are you ready?" It is going to happen! There will be a judgment day for each of us. It is fast approaching! Are you ready if it happens today?

It really saddens my heart during those times of false predictions how people were reacting to Jesus's coming back. Even though I knew the predictions were false, it still hurt to see how people made fun of that glorious day. This is something that should not be taken lightly. The same thing happened back during the day of Noah. God told him to build an ark and prepare for the end of the earth as they knew it. Can you imagine the ridicule that Noah went through with all of the people?

When the door of the ark closed, no one else was allowed to enter. They had been warned, but no one took heed except Noah and his immediate family. Take heed this day, and start looking upward for your redemption draws near.

Life's Journey Application

How can you prepare for the coming of the Lord? Are you ready and waiting for Jesus? The final door is getting ready to close. Don't take it lightly. Prepare now! Make yourself ready for your eternal life with Jesus.

. . . .

It's Almost Time for the Messiah's Return

Are you ready? Are you ready for the Messiah to return to take His children home? If you are not, then do not delay any longer! Jesus may come before you finish reading this page. He may come tonight, next

Tuesday, or even next year. You see, we don't know exactly when He will return on the cloud of glory, but I know He is coming!

Many years ago, God gave me a vision of a huge white watch. It was a vision of time ticking here on this earth. Time is ticking. Are you ready? Are you ready for the Messiah's entrance? Take a good look around you; prophecies are being fulfilled right before our eyes.

I believe that we are now in the time of the final outpouring of the Holy Spirit. We must begin to use our time to develop our personal relationship with Jesus. There will come a day when nothing else matters but the relationship we have with Him. There will be a day, whether it is from physical death or the rapture, when we will stand in front of Him as He opens the book of remembrance. He will locate your page and focus on your name. What will He find? Will He say, "Come in, My good and faithful servant, or depart from Me, I never knew you." Think for just a moment. What exactly will be written on your page?

Matthew 24:36 (NKJV) reads, "But of that day and hour no one knows not even the angels of Heaven, but My Father only." If we knew two days in advance that Jesus was coming, we all would make the necessary arrangements. We must be prepared at all times. He tells me always to be prepared. Revelation 22:12–13 (NKJV) tells us, "And behold I am coming quickly, and My reward is with Me, to give to everyone according to his works. I am the Alpha and the Omega, the Beginning and the End, the First and the Last."

All that mattered, matters no more ...because Jesus has come! Don't be left here!

Life's Journey Application

Are you prepared for His return? You must make the necessary preparations before the departure. I feel urgency in the air! He is coming back for a spotless church, ones that have their hearts right with Him! The trumpet is ready-set-poised to be blown. Are you ready?

. . . .

Hearing the Sound of Hooves

I believe within my heart Jesus is coming soon!

Hear the footsteps. Hear the horse's hooves pounding. Jesus is coming. Jesus is coming. Heartbeat pounds to sound of hooves! God's footsteps as described in 2 Chronicles 14:15 (NKJV), "as soon as you hear the sound of marching in the tops of the popular trees, move out to the battle, because that will mean God has gone out in front of you to strike the Philistine Army."

I believe God wants us to know, just like when he went before King David in battle, He will go before us. The battle is His. The victories are from Him. A final victory is coming for all the saints. He is coming. His footsteps are being heard across this land. Listen. God goes before you. Hear His footsteps as He prepares His army!

Hear the horses' hooves pounding. Horses' hooves signify truth to the ultimate degree. His truth is pounding! His truth is mounted up and galloping!

Heartbeat—hear the heartbeat of the spirit! The heartbeat of God is pounding ever so hard! Our hearts are being made ready with the horses' hooves (truth of God).

Listen to the footsteps. Prepare because Jesus is coming.

Life's Journey Application

The time is so close to the prophecy of Jesus returning to being fulfilled. Start making yourself ready for that day. There should be excitement, not fear, about this day. So if you are experiencing some fear, I believe that you need to strengthen your relationship with Jesus.

. . . .

Chapter 5 – Self-Evaluation

1. How are you preparing for the coming of Jesus?

2. Have you changed anything in your life to prepare for this day?

3. This best way to start preparing is to: read your Bible, pray, praise God, deepen your relationship with Jesus, make sure that you have asked for forgiveness, and find a church that preaches the Word of God. In making these a lifestyle, you will be truly living for Jesus.

See you in heaven!

****

Chapter 5—Notes

****

Printed in the United States
By Bookmasters